Johannine Faith
and Liberating Community

Johannine Faith
and Liberating Community

David Rensberger

The Westminster Press
Philadelphia

Scripture quotations in this work are the author's own translation.

Book design by Gene Harris

First edition

Published by The Westminster Press®
Philadelphia, Pennsylvania

PRINTED IN THE UNITED STATES OF AMERICA

9 8 7 6 5 4 3 2 1

Library of Congress Cataloging-in-Publication Data

Rensberger, David K.
  Johannine faith and liberating community / David Rensberger. — 1st ed.
     p.   cm.
  Bibliography: p.
  Includes indexes.
  ISBN 0-664-25041-6 (pbk.)

  1. Bible. N.T. John—Criticism, interpretation, etc.
2. Sociology, Biblical. 3. Liberation theology. I. Title.
BS2615.2.R39 1988
226'.5067—dc19   88-10052
                                     CIP

To my colleagues and students

at the

Interdenominational Theological Center

from whom I have learned so much

Contents

Abbreviations

Frequently Cited Works

Barrett, *Gospel According to St. John:* C. K. Barrett, *The Gospel According to St. John*, 2nd ed. (Philadelphia: Westminster Press, 1978).

Brown, *Community:* Raymond E. Brown, *The Community of the Beloved Disciple* (New York: Paulist Press, 1979).

Brown, *Gospel According to John:* Raymond E. Brown, ed. and tr., *The Gospel According to John*, 2 vols., AB 29, 29A (Garden City, N.Y.: Doubleday & Co., 1966, 1970).

Bultmann, *Gospel of John:* Rudolf Bultmann, *The Gospel of John: A Commentary* (Philadelphia: Westminster Press, 1971).

Cullmann, *Early Christian Worship:* Oscar Cullmann, *Early Christian Worship*, trans. A. Stewart Todd and James B. Torrance (Philadelphia: Westminster Press, 1953).

Cullmann, *Johanneische Kreis:* Oscar Cullmann, *Der johanneische Kreis* (Tübingen: J. C. B. Mohr [Paul Siebeck], 1975).

Dodd, *Historical Tradition:* C. H. Dodd, *Historical Tradition in the Fourth Gospel* (Cambridge: Cambridge University Press, 1963).

Dodd, *Interpretation:* C. H. Dodd, *The Interpretation of the Fourth Gospel* (Cambridge: Cambridge University Press, 1953).

Duke, *Irony:* Paul D. Duke, *Irony in the Fourth Gospel* (Atlanta: John Knox Press, 1985).

Haenchen, *John:* Ernst Haenchen, *John: A Commentary on the Gospel of John*, 2 vols., Hermeneia (Philadelphia: Fortress Press, 1984).

de Jonge, *Jesus:* Marinus de Jonge, *Jesus: Stranger from Heaven and Son of God*, SBLSBS 11 (Missoula, Mont.: Scholars Press, 1977).

Käsemann, *Testament:* Ernst Käsemann, *The Testament of Jesus: A Study of the Gospel of John in the Light of Chapter 17* (Philadelphia: Fortress Press, 1968).

Lindars, *Gospel of John:* Barnabas Lindars, *The Gospel of John*, NCBC (Grand Rapids, Mich.: Wm. B. Eerdmans Publishing Co., 1972).

Loisy, *Quatrième évangile:* Alfred Loisy, *Le quatrième évangile* (Paris: Picard, 1903).

Martyn, "Glimpses": J. Louis Martyn, "Glimpses into the History of the Johannine Community," in *The Gospel of John in Christian History*, by J. Louis Martyn, 90–121 (New York: Paulist Press, 1978).

Martyn, *History and Theology:* J. Louis Martyn, *History and Theology in the Fourth Gospel*, 2nd ed. rev. and enl. (Nashville: Abingdon Press, 1979).

Meeks, "Man from Heaven": Wayne A. Meeks, "The Man from Heaven in Johannine Sectarianism," *JBL* 91 (1972) 44–72.

Schnackenburg, *Gospel According to St John:* Rudolf Schnackenburg, *The Gospel According to St John*, 3 vols. (New York: Crossroad Publishing Co., 1982).

Smith, *Johannine Christianity:* D. Moody Smith, *Johannine Christianity: Essays on Its Setting, Sources, and Theology* (Columbia, S.C.: University of South Carolina Press, 1984).

Wengst, *Gemeinde:* Klaus Wengst, *Bedrängte Gemeinde und verherrlichter Christus: Der historische Ort des Johannesevangeliums als Schlüssel zu seiner Interpretation*, Biblisch-Theologische Studien 5, 2nd ed. (Neukirchen-Vluyn: Neukirchener Verlag, 1983).

Journals and Series

AB	Anchor Bible
BBB	Bonner biblische Beiträge
BETL	Bibliotheca ephemeridum theologicarum lovaniensium
BEvT	Beiträge zur evangelischen Theologie
BHT	Beiträge zur historischen Theologie
Bib	*Biblica*
BibLeb	*Bibel und Leben*
BSac	*Bibliotheca Sacra*
BTB	*Biblical Theology Bulletin*
BZ	*Biblische Zeitschrift*
CBQ	*Catholic Biblical Quarterly*
EvTh	*Evangelische Theologie*
ExpTim	*Expository Times*
JBL	*Journal of Biblical Literature*
JQR	*Jewish Quarterly Review*
JSNT	*Journal for the Study of the New Testament*
NCBC	New Century Bible Commentary
NovT	*Novum Testamentum*

NovTSup Novum Testamentum, Supplements
NRT   La nouvelle revue théologique
NTS   New Testament Studies
RelSRev Religious Studies Review
RevScRel Revue des sciences religieuses
SANT   Studien zum Alten und Neuen Testament
SBB   Stuttgarter biblische Beiträge
SBL   Society of Biblical Literature
SBLDS   SBL Dissertation Series
SBLMS   SBL Monograph Series
SBLSBS   SBL Sources for Biblical Studies
SBS   Stuttgarter Bibelstudien
SBT   Studies in Biblical Theology
SJLA   Studies in Judaism in Late Antiquity
SJT   Scottish Journal of Theology
SNTSMS   Society for New Testament Studies Monograph Series
SPB   Studia postbiblica
ThR   Theologische Rundschau
TLZ   Theologische Literaturzeitung
WMANT   Wissenschaftliche Monographien zum Alten und Neuen
         Testament
ZNW   Zeitschrift für die neutestamentliche Wissenschaft
ZTK   Zeitschrift für Theologie und Kirche

Preface

In my first semester at the Interdenominational Theological Center, I had the opportunity to teach a course on the gospel of John. The premise suggested in chapter 1 of this book became clear to me in outline as I prepared for that course, and in a sense I have been writing the book ever since.

But the actual task of putting various smaller studies together into book form was only undertaken during a sabbatical leave in the 1986–1987 academic year that gave me the freedom to do so. I am grateful to my colleagues at the ITC, including President James H. Costen and Dean David T. Shannon, for making this opportunity available and for their continued encouragement and support.

The sabbatical leave was funded by two grants: a Theological Scholarship and Research Grant from the Association of Theological Schools, and a Mellon Fund Strengthening the Humanities Program grant from the United Negro College Fund. To both of these agencies I express here my deepest appreciation.

The earliest form of chapters 1 and 6, and of other material now found scattered throughout the book, was presented as the Charles B. Copher Faculty Lectures at the ITC, March 12–13, 1985. I wish to thank those responsible for its acceptance into the Copher Lectures series. The writing of these lectures did much to organize and deepen my thinking and so helped me greatly toward this book. Moreover, their reception and criticism by their first hearers, including the respondent, Professor Noel Erskine of the Candler School of Theology, Emory University, were a great source of encouragement and help. The lectures as originally delivered have been published in the *Journal of the Interdenominational Theological Center* 13 (1985–1986) 155–193.

An earlier form of chapter 5 appeared in the *Journal of Biblical Literature* 103 (1984) 395–411. It was originally delivered as a paper at the Southeast Regional Meeting of the Society of Biblical Literature, as also was the original form of chapter 3. Chapter 4 was first read to the annual national meeting of the Society in Atlanta in November 1986. I wish to acknowledge here the helpful comments received on these occasions from the scholars present.

I wrote the first draft of chapter 7 as a participant in the June 1987 Biblical Theology Seminar sponsored by the Institute of Mennonite Studies at the Associated Mennonite Biblical Seminaries in Elkhart, Indiana. The memory of that peaceful place and cordial fellowship will long remain with me. I am deeply grateful to the members of the Seminar, and in particular to its organizer, the director of the IMS, Professor Willard M. Swartley, for providing a context that was both critical and encouraging in which to shape the concluding portion of these studies.

All the people mentioned above have been very helpful to me as this book has developed, and I am thankful too to Dr. Cynthia L. Thompson of The Westminster Press for her encouragement and good advice along the way. Obviously, though, it is I myself who must bear the burden of any failings the book retains. I know that at a number of points, particularly in chapter 6, I have ventured into areas outside the traditional confines of Johannine studies with what may seem an all-too-brash naïveté. I am aware of at least some of the criticisms that may be raised at such points, but the risks seem to me to be worthwhile in order to open up several areas of discussion whose possibility is only now beginning to become apparent. I do not by any means suppose that I have said the last word on such matters. On the contrary, I hope at times to have said only the first of many words that need saying and to have left a great deal of room for further development and debate.

No task such as this could be undertaken without the support of one's family, and I thank my wife, Sharon, and my daughters, Miranda and Felicity, for their understanding of the amount of time taken from them by it.

The dedication of this book is most sincerely meant. The unusual environment of the Interdenominational Theological Center and the unusual opportunity given me to share in the life of the black church and to witness the ongoing development of black theology have furnished the indispensable matrix in which studies such as these could be nurtured. I am truly grateful to the ITC community, without which this work would not have developed as it has.

1
The New Era
in Johannine Interpretation

By an ancient and widespread habit, we are accustomed to think of the gospel of John as the "spiritual gospel." In comparison with Matthew, Mark, and Luke, John is held to present a more inward or theologically profound side of the New Testament interpretation of Jesus, or even of the teaching of Jesus himself. Hence this gospel is often regarded as either the best introduction to or the most sublime meditation on what Christians believe about Jesus. As such, it is commonly given the role of leading individuals to faith in Christ or of deepening their communion with him or their understanding of his significance. What it may have to say about social relations among individuals, much less among groups of people, tends to get relegated to a rather remote subsection of a late chapter of our thinking about John, under the rubric "Love one another."

Recent developments in the study of the Fourth Gospel have the potential of bringing about a revolutionary change in this situation. By revealing as never before the social and historical setting in which this gospel was written, and the conflicts in which the Johannine community was involved, they have opened up new possibilities in the interpretation of John, some of which have scarcely been available in the entire nineteen hundred years since the book first appeared. They offer us the opportunity to reach back behind the time when John came to be understood as the "spiritual gospel" and to see more nearly the whole range of meanings that would have been apparent to its first generation of readers.

In part, these developments are related to broader tendencies in New Testament study generally.[1] The letters of Paul, for instance, are being subjected to an analysis that is deliberately and self-consciously "sociological," even if the methods and results are of necessity not always those which professional sociologists might expect. In Paul's case, however, the polemic situations in which his letters were written

are self-evident and have long been exploited in theological interpretation, although the sociological approach to them has not appeared
until quite recently. With John, the actual conflicts are below the
surface of the text, as we shall see, and it is only now becoming
possible to hope that knowledge of them will bear fruit for the study of
Johannine theology comparable to that in the Pauline field. Moreover,
the beginning of a sociological approach to the New Testament is
related to the advance of a number of pressing social concerns to the
forefront of theological discussion in many areas of the church today.
Is it possible that John too can be brought to bear on these issues,
much as the teaching and life of Jesus and the letters of Paul have
already been brought to bear on them?

To set out the present position in Johannine studies, it is necessary
to start by indicating something of the traditional understanding of
the gospel of John as well as the general situation of critical Johannine
scholarship leading up to the developments in question. My intention
is to give only a survey, not a detailed history of research, and in the
process to emphasize one trend in particular.[2] There will be many
significant areas of Johannine research that will receive only brief
mention, if any, which does not imply that they do not also contribute
to our contemporary understanding of the Fourth Gospel. In particular, I will be concerned with developments that lie more within the
interests of historical-critical approaches to the New Testament than
within those of the various literary-critical methodologies that have
recently come to the fore. These methodologies have a considerable
value, especially for so carefully constructed a work as John, and I do
not think they need necessarily be divorced from the social questions pursued here.[3] Indeed, some of the detailed studies later in
this book, especially in chapter 5, will have a significant literary
component, though one that is more akin to a close reading than,
say, to a structuralist analysis. The new literary approach to John is
a factor in the transformation of our understanding. However, the
changes that seem to me the most truly revolutionary in their import center more on the historical setting of the Fourth Gospel and
its readers.

Changing Approaches to John

The conception of John as the "spiritual gospel" began very early in
Christian history. It is first attested around 200 C.E. by Clement of
Alexandria, who, as quoted by the church historian Eusebius, reported
the tradition that John wrote a "spiritual gospel" in the knowledge
that the "physical" data were already contained in the other gospels.[4]

Earlier still, we find the Valentinian gnostic Heracleon giving a highly symbolic interpretation of the Fourth Gospel, treating it very much as a "spiritual" document.[5] It seems likely, in fact, that by the middle of the second century the actual circumstances and controversies that gave birth to the individual writings of the New Testament had been almost entirely forgotten. The books were being interpreted in the light of the new needs and rapidly developing theologies of the various Christian communions, while the impulses that originally called them forth were quickly fading into an already distant past. Even in the case of Paul it is rare to meet a Christian writer in the second century who interprets the epistles within anything resembling their author's own frame of reference.[6] As for the gospels, both their form and their content worked to direct interest even more strongly away from the circumstances of their composition, which (apart from brief traditional notices mainly regarding authorship) received relatively little attention until the rise of modern critical scholarship.

In these conditions, it is not surprising that John came to be regarded as the "spiritual" gospel. The book, after all, insists that the spirit is what gives life, while the flesh is of no avail, and that the words of Jesus it presents are spirit and life (John 6:63); and also that God, who is spirit, desires only worship that is "in spirit and in truth" (4:24). The haunting profundity of its opening words and the elusive character of its language, whose meaning so often seems to be finally in one's grasp the moment before it slips irretrievably away, combine to make this gospel itself seem very much like the Spirit, which "blows where it will . . . but you do not know where it comes from or whither it is going" (3:8). It thus lay ready to hand to explain its manifest differences from the other three canonical gospels by conceiving of it as a supplement to them, the "spiritual" or "theological" gospel, the gospel of *Logos* rather than *sarx*, of Word rather than flesh.[7]

The effect of this conception has been to focus the interpretation of John, even more than that of other biblical books, on its *ideas*. The significance of John is felt almost as a matter of course to lie in its system of thought, its theology. The abstract language of the Fourth Gospel easily leads the interpreter to deal with it as an exercise in abstraction and to seek out the basic principles around which the system of abstractions behind it might be organized. This is certainly appropriate, and may be inevitable; but it does tend to obscure and delay the recognition that other realities, of a more concrete social and historical nature, may be at least equally as important as ideology in explaining the Fourth Gospel.

In the modern period, of course, historical questions of a number of kinds have been raised about John. Indeed, it is precisely the historicity of John, its historical reliability, that has been the most thoroughly debated issue in Johannine scholarship. Through the first half of the twentieth century, it was generally assumed that John had made use of Mark, and perhaps Luke as well, as source material for his work.[8] To the extent that his account differed from theirs, it became necessary to regard it as, if the more spiritual, ipso facto the less historical. John's historical accuracy has always had many defenders, but such an obvious discrepancy as its placing of the cleansing of the Temple at the beginning of Jesus' work rather than at the end, as Mark does, can really be accounted for only by saying that one of them is historically right and the other is wrong; and on this matter, as on others, the decision for most scholars has gone in favor of Mark.[9] But differences in chronology are not the core of the problem. It is the Johannine presentation of Jesus himself that is the really insuperable difficulty. The variances from Jesus' teaching as the Synoptics present it—the long, repetitious harangues instead of parables and short sayings, the focus on Jesus' own relationship to God rather than on the kingdom of God and on ethics—are too well known to detail here.[10] Estimates of the extent to which a historical nucleus might lie behind this or that saying or incident varied considerably, but again by the middle of this century it had long since been concluded that John could not be used as a source for historical knowledge of Jesus in the same way as the Synoptics.[11] The gospel's authorship was likewise a matter of dispute. In general, the more remote it seemed from the historical Jesus, the less likely it seemed that the apostle John the son of Zebedee could have written it.

Literary questions formed a significant part of the inquiry concerning John during this period. Numerous studies attempted to discover an earlier book behind the Fourth Gospel as we now have it, one that was subjected to rewritings, interpolations, supplementations, and rearrangements, discerned in various ways by different scholars based on discontinuities in language and style or narrative sequence.[12] Investigations of John's sources were made as well. Besides Mark (and perhaps Luke), other sources were also invoked to help explain the gospel's peculiarities.[13] On the one hand, this applies to the Passion narrative; and on the other, Rudolf Bultmann forcefully advanced the idea of a "signs" source that contained the miracles of Jesus found in John and a gnostic "discourse" source that furnished the basis for the distinctive speeches of the Johannine Jesus.[14]

Both John's historicity and its literary development, however, were long studied in close connection with the background of its language and thought. For it seemed quite clear that the Logos conception, the strong dualism, and much else besides could not be explained on the basis of the Palestinian Judaism of the time of Jesus. It was just this which seemed most unhistorical about John and which therefore was thought to have entered into its presentation of Jesus as the result of influences outside the gospel tradition. Moreover, as I have observed, it was the *ideas* of the "spiritual gospel" that always formed the primary object of its interpretation. Therefore its historical investigation as well inevitably gravitated toward the history of its ideas, whose origins were sought in a variety of directions. The thinking of Paul was often regarded as one influence, despite the absence of really Pauline language: to some, Paul seemed the natural bridge from Jesus to John.[15] Other influences seemed even more obvious.[16] The first of these was always Greek philosophy in general and the highly Hellenized Jewish philosophy of Philo of Alexandria in particular. Early in this century, the effort was made to trace mystical elements in the thought of John to the Hellenistic mystery religions. At the same time, gnosticism was also being exploited for its contributions to interpreting the Fourth Gospel. Primarily it was the Hermetic literature that was seen as the most promising in this regard, but Bultmann and others pointed to Mandaean gnostic texts as offering the clue to understanding John. All these influences came from outside the realm of Palestinian Judaism. Yet there were those who sought to show that John's peculiarities could be explained from within that realm, by pointing to parallels in rabbinic literature or in Jewish mystical writings.[17]

In all of this, we see how strongly the perception that in John it was the ideas that mattered determined the direction of critical study. By the early 1950s it was widely conceded that John was late in date and historically unreliable in comparison to the Synoptics. But the primary basis for this conclusion remained the fact that John represented a *theological* development that went well beyond theirs. Literary criticism played a strong role of its own, but essentially to explain John meant to explain his thought and its origin. The study of the Fourth Gospel focused on theology in the abstract and so remained an undertaking in the history of ideas. C. H. Dodd's classic work on the interpretation of the Fourth Gospel is the enduring and indispensable monument to this endeavor.[18] Likewise, on the deepest level, Bultmann's Protestant-existentialist interpretation stands as the modern climax of the tradition that looks on John as the "spiritual gospel," for no other contemporary commentator has succeeded in drawing the reader so powerfully away from the "physical" data of history toward inward encounter with God.[19]

In the last thirty years, however, advances have been made that challenge not only this or that critical conclusion but the dominance of this tradition as a whole.[20] The first of these has to do with the background of the Fourth Gospel. The discovery of the Dead Sea

Scrolls revealed a Hebrew- and Aramaic-speaking Jewish sect in first-century Palestine that expressed itself in much of the same dualistic, exclusivistic, and "inward" terminology as John. Thus at one stroke the need to locate John's background entirely outside Jewish Palestine fell away. Already in 1929, Hugo Odeberg had begun to draw on Jewish mystical texts in interpreting John,[21] and in more recent times the importance for Johannine interpretation of these and other forms of "heterodox Judaism" (however vaguely this term may often be understood) has rightly come to the fore.[22] It is not that John can now be claimed as "Jewish" and not "Hellenistic"; rather, we now know how deeply Judaism and Hellenism had interpenetrated, even in Palestine.[23] Clearly also there remains much in John that cannot be explained solely in Palestinian terms. But the need for a long period of contact with Hellenistic philosophy, gnosticism, and mystery religions to account for the Fourth Gospel now seems far less than before. We are still in the realm of the history of ideas here, but the effect of these discoveries was to suggest that conclusions long regarded as assured were in fact open to question.[24] At the same time, attention was drawn to the need for renewed investigation of Johannine *origins*.

The second area of significant advance has to do with the relation of John to the Synoptic gospels. Already in 1938, P. Gardner-Smith had argued that John was not dependent on Mark or any of the Synoptics but that he and they drew independently on related traditions.[25] This viewpoint has gradually gained widespread acceptance, until it is now the dominant one, though arguments for the opposite position remain.[26] A further turning point came in 1963, however, with C. H. Dodd's volume on historical tradition in the Fourth Gospel.[27] It was Dodd's fundamental methodological insight in this study that the tools of form criticism applied by Bultmann and others to the Synoptics could equally well be applied to John. By doing so, he was able to make a convincing demonstration that the materials in John belong to a tradition of their own, not dependent on the Synoptics. Though radically reshaped by the author of the Fourth Gospel, this special tradition goes back ultimately to the same type of oral transmission as the traditions behind the Synoptics. Dodd's result leads to various further conclusions. For Dodd himself, it meant that the material in John could once again be considered valuable in seeking the historical facts about Jesus. Most scholars have felt that Dodd pressed this point too far, not recognizing that the mere fact that something in John goes back to a tradition does not make it "historical." But Dodd also opened up the possibility of studying the form history of the Johannine material and comparing this history with that of the Synoptics, much of which still waits to be done. Above all, Dodd liberated Johannine studies from the need to focus on written sources, whether the Synoptic gospels or Bultmann's hypothetical "signs" and "discourse" documents. A Johannine tradition had now been posited that could be investigated as an independent entity with its own origin and life setting.[28]

This new possibility was to be exploited in various ways by numerous scholars, two of whom in particular may be mentioned at this point.[29] Raymond Brown combined a literary analysis of the continuities and discontinuities in the gospel with the notion of an independent Johannine stream of tradition. As a result, he proposed a lengthy and complex development from oral tradition about Jesus; through its shaping within a particular Christian community, giving it its peculiarly Johannine character and content; to the writing of the gospel, and its subsequent reediting to include material from the tradition that had previously been left out.[30] Somewhat similarly, Barnabas Lindars suggested that the origins of the Fourth Gospel lay in a diverse body of traditions and short collections of material about Jesus, which served as the basis for homilies in the Johannine style and character, these homilies being then reworked by their author to form the gospel itself, in a first and an expanded second edition, which was later subjected to a variety of small supplementations.[31] Both Brown and Lindars thus see John as the outcome of a complicated process of composition and redaction, in a way reminiscent of earlier literary theories; but both regard the main features of the gospel as the product of a single author's reflection on a tradition essentially independent of the Synoptics. Lindars allows for more diversity at the start of the process, including more contact with Synoptic tradition and less likelihood of a unified apostolic eyewitness at the beginning. Nevertheless both scholars clearly envision the Johannine tradition and its development into a written gospel as an independent process within the history of early Christianity, having only limited contact with the traditions that produced the Synoptic gospels.

The significance of this perception can hardly be overestimated. Theories of extensive pre-Johannine written sources continue to be relevant; in particular the work of Robert Fortna on the "signs" source has been influential,[32] and there are those who still defend the dependence of John upon Mark.[33] But Dodd, Brown, Lindars, and others have shown that it is also possible to interpret the Fourth Gospel without reference to such sources. Although the complex theories of Brown and Lindars may never be proven in detail, they exemplify the contemporary focus on an independent body of Johannine traditions nurtured within a particular early Christian community, and it is this focus which has opened the way to developments in the study of John that must be seen as truly epoch-making.

The form-critical approach to the gospels carries with it the implication that the Christian community in which the traditions were shaped had a decisive impact on the formation and transformation of these traditional materials. Form criticism draws attention to the *Sitz im Leben* of the materials, that is, to their setting in the life of the early Christian community. It is concerned with the *function* served by the gospel traditions in the community's living encounter with its own mission and needs and with the world around it.[34] Though other forces were also at work, Dodd, in consistently applying form criticism to the Fourth Gospel for the first time, made it inevitable that the character and situation of the Johannine community would become a major object of investigation.

The next crucial step forward was made by J. Louis Martyn. In his book on history and theology in the Fourth Gospel, Martyn set out to discover whether the gospel of John is in any way a "response to contemporary events and issues" in the daily life of the Christian community in which its author lived.[35] He concluded that John was written late in the first century in a community of Jewish Christians who were in the process of being marked off and expelled from the Jewish community by means of the Benediction against Heretics that had recently been introduced into the synagogue liturgy in their city. It was a traumatic time of decision for Christians who had maintained their allegiance both to the Jewish religion and synagogue fellowship and to the messiahship of Jesus and the new Christian group. John's gospel was written for those who were faced with this decision and explores the communal and theological dimensions of it by means of a "two-level drama" wherein the stories about Jesus reflect also the experience and convictions of the author and his church.[36] Such a situation of conflict has of course been posited by others independently of Martyn.[37] But by presenting the hypothesis in such detail and by linking it strongly to the exegesis of the gospel, Martyn succeeded in drawing attention to this as *the* setting within which the distinctive Johannine tradition about Jesus took form as the Fourth Gospel.

Subsequent studies have fully confirmed the rightness of this basic insight. While few have accepted Martyn's delineation of the action behind the Fourth Gospel in all its details, the fundamental conception that he outlined has been elaborated in a variety of directions and has become the cornerstone of much current Johannine research. Brown, in dialogue with Martyn, has worked out a complete, if highly speculative, history of the Johannine community from its beginnings to its dissipation in the second century.[38] Wayne Meeks explored the significance of John's communal setting for understanding the pattern of Johannine christological language,[39] and Marinus de Jonge went on to make a wide-ranging series of theological and historical probes into the Fourth Gospel on the basis of the suggested communal context.[40]

D. Moody Smith, besides a number of articles on John's sources, theology, and relation to the Synoptics, produced an admirable summary of scholarship on the existence and nature of a distinctively Johannine form of early Christianity.[41] A host of other studies have also appeared that take this proposed community situation of John as their essential presupposition.[42]

What may we say about the present position in Johannine studies as a result of these developments? So far as the historicity of John is concerned, the recognition of Dodd and others that John derives from a stream of tradition parallel to that of the Synoptics puts it on a more nearly equal footing with them.[43] We may now be more willing to see behind some incident or saying found only in John a datum of tradition going back ultimately to the historical Jesus. However, this realization should not obscure the enormous distance that still must be traveled from John backward to Jesus. The new clarity regarding John's milieu and its influence on the gospel afforded by Martyn and others makes us aware again of this distance, and however much light the Dead Sea Scrolls may have shed on the possibility of "mystical" teaching in Jewish Palestine, the Jesus of John still differs from the Jesus of the Synoptics, so that the question of historicity still must be decided on other grounds than mere parallel-gathering. Our primary object in studying this gospel must remain the intention of John, not the intention of Jesus.

It is in fact the recovery of the historical setting of the Johannine gospel and its tradition that is the truly pivotal advance now being made. Robert Kysar calls this "the lasting contribution of the last quarter of the twentieth century to Johannine scholarship,"[44] and Jürgen Becker speaks of a breakthrough to new perceptions in the quest for the history of the Johannine community.[45] I believe it is possible to emphasize even more strongly yet the historic nature of this breakthrough.

Ernst Käsemann once deplored the lack of information about John's historical background, "information which would determine our understanding of the whole book and not merely of individual details."[46] Käsemann himself sought to supply this lack by beginning from John's Christology to explain the book's historical situation.[47] In fact, as we shall see, exactly the reverse is the more illuminating procedure: once the historical background has been partially filled in by the use of other resources, the Christology can be far better understood. Käsemann was absolutely correct to stress what is distinctive about the Fourth Gospel, rather than seeking to harmonize it with the others, and to eschew any facile attempt at balance through a premature appeal to paradox or dialectic.[48] However, his starting point led him inevitably to the notion that the Johannine Christology is a dogmatic of "naive docetism" focusing on the glory of Christ to the neglect of his true humanity.[49] Starting from the communal history as worked out by Martyn and others, we can now see that the Johannine emphasis on Jesus' glory arises out of the situation in which the book was written, wherein the point at issue was precisely the messiahship of Jesus and its significance. John's opponents did not doubt that Jesus was truly human; what John had to show was Jesus' heavenly origin, and it was this which led him to the Christology that does indeed have "docetic" features when seen apart from its original context and purpose.[50] It is just the knowledge of this context that we may now hope will lead toward the understanding that Käsemann sought. The controversies in which the Johannine materials were forged were virtually lost to sight from the second century onward, when John came to be regarded as the "spiritual gospel." Their rediscovery and promotion to so prominent a place in research at a time when biblical and theological studies may be peculiarly prepared to respond to them could prove to be of extraordinary significance in the history of the interpretation of the Fourth Gospel. Obviously not all the details of John's historical situation have been recovered in any agreed-upon way; perhaps all the details never will be. Yet enough has been done to enable further exploration to proceed with confidence.

The full implications of this new position largely remain to be worked out. To date, most research has concentrated on delineating the Johannine community, its situation, and its history, and on locating the traces of these things in the text. Besides the studies already noted, we may mention, as examples, the work of Fernando Segovia, who sees communal schisms lying behind the redaction of the gospel;[51] D. Bruce Woll, who finds reflected in John 13 and 14 a conflict within the community over charismatic authority;[52] and Rodney Whitacre, who compares the use of polemic and the communal situation in the gospel with those in the Johannine epistles.[53] In Germany, we may note especially the study by Klaus Wengst, who not only lays out the Johannine community's historical situation but also goes on to draw conclusions for John's theological interpretation.[54] Otherwise the focus of German scholarship has tended to be especially on the theological history of the community and its bearing on Johannine literary criticism.[55] As examples, one may cite the studies of Hartwig Thyen[56] and Georg Richter.[57] "Theology" here means primarily *Christology*, for both in this country and in Europe the history of the Johannine community has been closely linked to christological developments—from lower to higher, from high to docetic—and the conflicts and schisms claimed to have resulted from them.

Yet we have barely begun to realize what the awareness of John's communal setting may mean for our understanding and appropriation of Johannine theology. Knowledge of the conflicts that stimulated the writing of the Fourth Gospel could enrich our theological understanding of it in a manner similar to what has long been true of Paul. We may also look for a shift in the context within which theological statements are interpreted, from the realm of the abstract and "eternal" to that of theology's emergence out of the actual life of a particular community in a particular situation. Something like this transfer has been under way for some time in various areas of biblical studies, but the dialectic between theology and communal experience now seems so pronounced in John that Johannine studies may yet take the lead in this process. I do not mean to imply that the time to pursue the classical lines of Johannine interpretation, with their focus on Johannine theology, is at an end. Rather, the theological and the "sociological" interpretation of John must now begin to feed and to condition each other. It may well be that a new era in the theological understanding of John is opening up precisely in our new awareness of the social background of this gospel. For we are now in a position to ask about the social implications of Johannine thought, and in the case of the "spiritual gospel," this, I believe, may rightly be considered revolutionary.

The Johannine Community

The description of the Johannine community's situation and character given here will not be as detailed as many of the studies that have been mentioned above. This is because I do not believe it is possible to be confident of as much detail as some writers do and also because I wish to offer at this point a generic or consensus portrait, one that could be regarded as generally agreed upon by most scholars in the field.

As I have indicated, the determinative factor in the milieu of the Johannine Christian community was its conflict with the synagogue. We must think at first of a group of Christians still entirely within the fold of the Jewish community. It is possible that the affiliations of some members of this group were with Essene-like or other "mystical" or dualistic tendencies in ancient Judaism rather than with a more ordinary piety.[58] The group also possessed traditions about Jesus and used them to nourish its faith and life. Its confession of Jesus as Messiah, however, brought it into growing tension with the authorities of the Jewish community. Evidently the Pharisees had come to power in the group's environment after the First Revolt in 70 C.E., and they now undertook an effort to suppress dissident elements within the community.[59] In this process, Jewish Christians were especially subject to pressure, and for the Johannine group the result was expulsion from the synagogue community altogether. Particular factors in the makeup of Johannine Christianity at this point—the nature of its christological confession above all, but perhaps also the presence in it of "heterodox" Jewish elements, or its relation to Samaritans and Gentiles—may have helped bring about the rupture.

The exact mechanism employed in this expulsion has recently come under some discussion. Martyn proposed that the twelfth benediction of the synagogue liturgy's Eighteen Benedictions, the "Benediction against Heretics" (*Birkat ha-Minim*), introduced under the authority of Rabban Gamaliel II at Jamnia, was being used in such a way that Johannine Christians had either to expose their faith in Jesus or invoke a curse on themselves during the synagogue prayers.[60] A number of scholars have challenged this claim, however.[61] They point out, among other factors, that John does not refer to synagogue *prayers*; that the exact wording of this benediction was, like the others, not yet fixed in the first century; that the term "heretics" might include, but was not limited to, Christians, while a specific reference to Jewish Christians was not introduced into the benediction until perhaps the fourth century; and that the authority of the rabbis at Jamnia, even if they did create a benediction to be used against Jewish Christians, may not have been widely acknowledged for quite some time. Thus it has come to seem doubtful that the Benediction against Heretics was the means by which the Johannine Christians were excluded from the synagogue fellowship. This, however, does not invalidate the essence of Martyn's proposal that the Johannine Christians were being or had been expelled from the synagogue. The claim is not that *all* Christians were being so treated; it may have been, rather, a local phenomenon in the Johannine environment. Nevertheless, whatever the means employed and whatever the role, if any, of rabbinic decrees emanating from Jamnia, it seems incontrovertible from the thrice-repeated reference in John 9:22; 12:42; and 16:2 that the Johannine community experienced such an expulsion, and from the way in which they are treated throughout the gospel (e.g., John 1:24; 4:1; 12:42) that the Pharisees were perceived as the authorities behind it.[62] We may know less than we would like about the details, but it is surely correct to give this experience a central role in understanding the background of the Fourth Gospel.

Thus the Johannine group was faced with a crisis, as those who openly acknowledged their faith were expelled, while others strove through secrecy to maintain their standing within the Jewish community. It is important to realize both the dimensions and the results of this crisis. The Christians who were expelled would have been cut off from much that had given identity and structure to their lives.

Expulsion would have meant social ostracism and thus the loss of relationship with family and friends, and perhaps economic dislocation as well.[63] It would certainly have meant religious dislocation. The synagogue meetings, the public liturgy, the festivals and observances were all now denied them, and the authoritative interpretation of the sacred scripture itself was in the hands of their opponents. What was threatened was thus the entire universe of shared perceptions, assumptions, beliefs, ideals, and hopes that had given meaning to their world within Judaism.

As a result of this loss, the group seems to have turned inward upon itself. Its own (Jewish-)Christian traditions and beliefs, its own fellowship, now became the source of a new sacred universe and a new social context. A growing isolation and even alienation from outsiders apparently came to characterize the group. It could now think of "the Jews" as such as a foreign and hostile body, representative of "the world" at large.[64] Because of this alienation from Judaism, and perhaps from society in general—the well-known Johannine hostility to "the world"—the question whether the Johannine community ought to be regarded as a "sect" has come to be rather widely debated. We may digress here briefly to consider it.

Some scholars—for instance, Wayne Meeks—find the term "sectarian" appropriate for John;[65] others—for instance, Raymond Brown—do not.[66] To a considerable extent it is a matter of definition: thus Brown confines the discussion of sectarianism to the breaking of communion with other Christians.[67] But in fact it is the attitude toward Judaism and the outside world as a whole that seems most sectarian in John's gospel. While I have no wish to enter fully into sociological debates about what constitutes a "sect," we may cite the work of Bryan Wilson as an example of one widely accepted model of sectarianism.[68] In Wilson's terms, Johannine Christianity would probably be classified as an introversionist sect in that it "sees the world as irredeemably evil" and seeks to renounce it and establish a separated community. Clearly, as we shall see in subsequent chapters, "the community" in John "itself becomes the source and seat of all salvation. Explicitly this prospect of salvation is only for those who belong."[69] Yet, for John, the world is perhaps not quite irredeemably evil, nor is the community quite exclusively "preoccupied with its own holiness and its means of insulation from the wider society."[70] Unlike Wilson's introversionist type, and like his conversionist and revolutionist types, John "demands public expression in testifying to 'the truth,'" and apparently still hopes for new members.[71] The revolutionist type corresponds very closely to the Jewish eschatological apocalypticism that forms part of the background of John as of early Christianity as a whole.[72] In common with the conversionists, for John "the objective world will not change but the acquisition of a new subjective orientation to it will itself be salvation"; and in the gospel as we have it, there are both "the promise of a change in external reality at some future time" and "the prospect of the individual's transfer to another sphere." The requirement of a conversion *experience*, however, which Wilson stresses, is absent from John.[73] We thus see that, as Wilson emphasizes, these categories are ideal types, to any one of which any actual sectarian movement will at most approximate; but the usefulness of such a typology of sectarianism in approaching the Fourth Gospel is also clear.[74]

Thomas Johnson has in fact used twelve features commonly identified by sociologists of religion as characteristic of sectarian groups to demonstrate that Johannine Christianity does indeed adequately fulfill contemporary sociological definitions of a sect.[75] Of these twelve, we may mention in particular the rejection of the world; a claim to a unique or special truth; voluntary membership based on special religious experience or knowledge; intimate fellowship; and a dualistic view of reality.[76] Given the configuration of sectarian traits we have seen, and Johnson's demonstration in particular, it seems unavoidable that we regard the Johannine community as a sect, at least in relation to Judaism, if not also in relation to other Christians. We may think of the Johannine community, then, as a sectarian group of Jewish Christian origin, one that has distinctly introversionist features but one that has not necessarily turned its back entirely on the possibility of mission to the world.

In this setting, a dualism perhaps already latent in the group's thinking came strongly to the fore. Their Christology also was involved: if it was their confession of Jesus that had caused them to be expelled from the synagogue, their expulsion drove them to an ever more radical confession of him. Jesus became the center of their new cosmos, the locus of all sacred things. Not only the messianic fulfillment of scripture but also judgment and eternal life, the religious observances now closed to them, and Deity itself were all centered on him. His rejection by the world symbolized their own alienation, and the correct confession of Jesus became for them the touchstone of truth. The failure of some Christian Jews in their environment to make this open and forthright confession evokes a sharp reproof from the Fourth Evangelist, as Martyn and Brown have shown; and Brown argues that the insistence on right confession led them into conflict with other Christian groups as well.[77] Thus the Pharisaic synagogue authorities are not the only opponents in the Fourth Gospel.

It was within this situation of conflict, crisis, and alienation that the Fourth Gospel was written, and against this background it must be understood. The community's traditions about Jesus were powerfully recast in this milieu, reflecting the influence both of forces outside mainstream Jewish piety and of the conflict with the synagogue. No doubt we may also see in the gospel the impact of some one particularly powerful theologian and literary artist who was primarily responsible for this recasting. (If we refer to this evangelist as "John," it is only for the sake of using a convenient and familiar name, not to imply a historical identification of the author.) This reshaping of an originally independent stream of tradition is what gave the Fourth Gospel its peculiar character, advancing its portrayal of Jesus ever farther from the earlier tradition toward a deeper understanding, in a process perceived by the community as the work of the Spirit of Truth (John 14:25–26; 16:12–15).

The Present Studies

This is the context within which our study of the gospel of John will proceed. Certain limitations of this context, and therefore of these studies themselves, need to be mentioned here. I have said little about developments in the Johannine community prior to the break with the synagogue and nothing about the period after the writing of the gospel. My intention is to focus on the time of the gospel's composition itself, which I view as most intimately related to the synagogue conflict. The later period, which evidently saw the rise of dissensions within the community, especially over Christology, will seldom come into view.[78] I have also avoided the subject of John's sources and their possible relation to the history of the community before the gospel was written. John may have had written sources at his disposal, particularly for the Passion narrative and perhaps also for the miracle stories or "signs." However, I am not as confident as some about our ability to reconstruct such sources and connect them and their redaction to theological history.[79] This reluctance is due mainly to what I can see of the work of the gospel's main author. John obviously exercised a sovereign freedom in the use of whatever sources he had, rearranging them as he saw fit and subjecting their content both to his own brilliantly focused vision and to his extraordinarily subtle and many-layered manner of expressing it. This means on the one hand that the quest for a source's exact wording and shape is made unusually difficult, and on the other it means that the finished gospel is sufficiently self-contained to be more than adequate as an object of study. I am also attracted by the possibility, cogently put forward by several scholars, that John is not primarily dependent on written sources at all but on oral traditions, perhaps indeed on homilies of his own composing.[80] I hope that this inattention to source criticism on my part will be compensated for by fresh insights in other areas.

I must also make one other clarification. I will be attempting a social analysis, or at least some observations regarding social realities behind the text. However, in keeping with a distinction that has very rightly been drawn by John Gager and Robin Scroggs, among others,[81] I do not classify my work as "sociological." A sociological study would include an effort to explain the observations on the basis of a theoretical model or models, which I do not intend to do. It would be worthwhile, I think, for those who are better acquainted with sociological theory than I am to attempt this, if it seems that enough data can be made available for the purpose.[82] My own aims will be more simply descriptive than explanatory, an attempt to enrich our understanding of John's purpose and theology by paying attention to the social circumstances surrounding the community for whom the gospel was written.

The present position in Johannine studies is characterized by a sense of discovery and by an exciting new set of questions. What is the significance, both for John's theology and for our own, of the conflicts so intimately bound up with the development of Johannine Christology; of the attention to group boundaries and cohesion that this milieu seems to have brought about; and of the evidently sectarian nature of the community that gave birth to one of the great documents of the founding years of Christianity? The new sensitivity to John's communal setting has added, if nothing else, a dimension of realism to the interpretation of the Fourth Gospel, a sense of actual lives being lived very much "in the world," even if by people who have become alienated from that which is "of the world." As we proceed to the study of individual passages and motifs in John, we will be guided by this realism and by the hope that the recovery at last of this gospel's social context and the history of the people from whose experience it emerged, and whose lives and faith it sought to nurture, will enable John to speak, in his demanding and arresting way, to our own history and lives.

NOTES

1. Cf. the essays collected by Norman K. Gottwald in *The Bible and Liberation: Political and Social Hermeneutics.*

2. Comprehensive surveys of Johannine research over the last twenty years may be found in Robert Kysar, *The Fourth Evangelist and His Gospel: An Examination of Contemporary Scholarship;* idem, "The Gospel of John in Current Research," *RelSRev* 9 (1983) 314–323; and the series of articles by Hartwig Thyen and Jürgen Becker, "Aus der Literatur zum Johannesevangelium," in *ThR* 39

(1974) 222–252; 40 (1975) 289–330; 42 (1977) 221–270; 43 (1978) 328–359; 44 (1979) 97–134; 47 (1982) 279–301, 305–347; and most recently by Becker, "Das Johannesevangelium im Streit der Methoden (1980–1984)," *ThR* 51 (1986) 1–78.

3. For instance, a study by Takashi Onuki (*Gemeinde und Welt im Johannesevangelium*) combines in a creative and powerful way a literary critical approach inspired by H. G. Gadamer and the type of understanding of the Johannine community and its significance under consideration here.

4. Eusebius, *Historia ecclesiastica* 6.14.5.

5. On Heracleon, and the gnostic interpretation of John in general, see Elaine H. Pagels, *The Johannine Gospel in Gnostic Exegesis: Heracleon's Commentary on John.*

6. See Andreas Lindemann, *Paulus im ältesten Christentum;* and David K Rensberger, "As the Apostle Teaches: The Development of the Use of Paul's Letters in Second-Century Christianity" (Ph.D. diss., Yale University, 1981).

7. So much so that Maurice F. Wiles could use this phrase as the title for his study of John's earliest interpreters: *The Spiritual Gospel: The Interpretation of the Fourth Gospel in the Early Church.* See in particular pp. 11–21.

8. W. F. Howard, *The Fourth Gospel in Recent Criticism and Interpretation* (4th ed. revised by C. K. Barrett), 130–131. See also the discussion by D. Moody Smith, "John and the Synoptics: Some Dimensions of the Problem," in Smith, *Johannine Christianity,* 145–152.

9. Howard, *Fourth Gospel,* 141–142; and see the commentaries.

10. See D. Moody Smith, "The Presentation of Jesus in the Fourth Gospel," in Smith, *Johannine Christianity,* 175–181.

11. Howard, *Fourth Gospel,* 213–227.

12. Ibid., 95–102, 166–169.

13. Cf. ibid., 133–137, 166–167.

14. Bultmann, *Gospel of John,* passim.

15. Howard, *Fourth Gospel,* 5, 36–37, 226.

16. Ibid., 144–159, 170–172.

17. E.g., Hugo Odeberg, *The Fourth Gospel Interpreted in Its Relation to Contemporaneous Religious Currents,* cited in Howard, *Fourth Gospel,* 49, 158–159, 206.

18. Dodd, *Interpretation.*

19. Bultmann, *Gospel of John;* and idem, *Theology of the New Testament,* 2:3–92.

20. The summary in Kysar, *Fourth Evangelist,* 267–276, confirms the essential points made here, though his book touches on many other topics as well. Cf. the other surveys cited in n. 2 above.

21. In Odeberg, *The Fourth Gospel Interpreted* (n. 17 above).

22. So, e.g., Cullmann, *Johanneische Kreis,* 30–40; D. Moody Smith, "Johannine Christianity," in Smith, *Johannine Christianity,* 26–31; and Brown, *Community,* 30, 34–47. See the survey in Kysar, *Fourth Evangelist,* 102–146.

23. This is the subject of the essay by Wayne A. Meeks, "'Am I a Jew?'—Johannine Christianity and Judaism," in *Christianity, Judaism and Other Greco-Roman Cults* (ed. Jacob Neusner), 1:163–186.

24. Cf. John A. T. Robinson, "The New Look on the Fourth Gospel," in *Twelve New Testament Studies,* by John A. T. Robinson, 94–106, esp. pp. 98–102.

25. P. Gardner-Smith, *Saint John and the Synoptic Gospels,* cited by C. K. Barrett in Howard, *Fourth Gospel,* 169, and by Robinson, "New Look," 96–98.

26. See the well-nuanced discussion in D. Moody Smith, "John and the Synoptics," in Smith, *Johannine Christianity,* 145–172.

27. Dodd, *Historical Tradition.*

28. Cf., already before Dodd's work, Robinson, "New Look," 104–106. In 1964, and without reference to Dodd's *Historical Tradition,* D. Moody Smith already saw an emerging consensus around a Johannine tradition independent of the Synoptics ("The Sources of the Gospel of John," in Smith, *Johannine Christianity,* 56–61; originally in *NTS* 10 [1964] 336–351).

29. For other studies, see the surveys by Kysar, *Fourth Evangelist,* 38–81; and idem, "Current Research," 315.

30. Brown, *Gospel According to John,* 1:xxxiv–xxxix.

31. Lindars, *Gospel of John,* 46–54; also idem, *Behind the Fourth Gospel,* esp. pp. 38–42, 43–60, 62–63, 73–77.

32. Robert T. Fortna, *The Gospel of Signs: A Reconstruction of the Narrative Source Underlying the Fourth Gospel.* Kysar notes other studies in his "Current Research," 315.

33. E.g., Barrett, *Gospel According to St. John,* 42–45.

34. See Rudolf Bultmann, *The History of the Synoptic Tradition,* 4; and Martin Dibelius, *From Tradition to Gospel,* 7.

35. Martyn, *History and Theology,* 18.

36. Ibid., 37–41, 60–62, and passim; cf. also Martyn, "Glimpses," 90–121.

37. Cf. Howard, *Fourth Gospel,* 59; and Kysar, *Fourth Evangelist,* 150–156.

38. Brown, *Community;* cf. Martyn's end of the dialogue in "Glimpses."

39. Meeks, "Man from Heaven."

40. Collected in de Jonge, *Jesus.*

41. The title essay in Smith, *Johannine Christianity,* in which volume the other studies are also collected.

42. Cf. Smith's title essay in Smith, *Johannine Christianity;* and Kysar, "Current Research." Jürgen Becker ("Aus der Literatur" [*ThR* 47] 306) regards this conception as a consensus position.

43. Cf. already Robinson, "New Look," 100–101.

44. Kysar, "Current Research," 318.

45. Becker, "Aus der Literatur" (*ThR* 47) 312.

46. Käsemann, *Testament,* 1.

47. Cf. ibid., 20–21, 24.

48. Ibid., 7–12.

49. Ibid., 23–26, and passim, especially in the second chapter.

50. So also Wengst, *Gemeinde,* 100–101.

51. Fernando Segovia, *Love Relationships in the Johannine Tradition: Agapê/Agapan in I John and the Fourth Gospel.*

52. D. Bruce Woll, *Johannine Christianity in Conflict: Authority, Rank, and Succession in the First Farewell Discourse.*

53. Rodney A. Whitacre, *Johannine Polemic: The Role of Tradition and Theology.*

54. Wengst, *Gemeinde.* Wengst's attempt to locate the Johannine communities precisely in the southern area of the kingdom of Agrippa II, east of the Sea of Galilee (ibid., 77–93), is certainly attractive but falls short of being fully persuasive.

55. Cf. Becker's formulation of the current situation of research in "Aus der Literature" (*ThR* 47) 305; and the survey in Wengst, *Gemeinde,* 18–28.

56. Hartwig Thyen, "Entwicklungen innerhalb der johanneischen Theologie und Kirche im Spiegel von Joh. 21 und der Lieblingsjüngertexte des Evangeliums," in *L'Evangile de Jean: Sources, rédaction, théologie* (ed. Marinus de Jonge), 269–273, 277–280, 293; cf. Thyen's surveys of research, "Aus der Literatur" (*ThR* 43) 340–341; and "Aus der Literatur" (*ThR* 44) 98.

57. Georg Richter, "Präsentische und futurische Eschatologie im 4. Evangelium," in *Studien zum Johannesevangelium,* by Georg Richter, 346–382; and idem, "Zum gemeindebildenden Element in den johanneischen Schriften," ibid., 383–414.

58. Cf. the references in n. 22 above.

59. Cf. Wengst, *Gemeinde,* 57, 62.

60. Martyn, *History and Theology,* 37–62.

61. E.g., Reuven Kimelman, *"Birkat Ha-Minim* and the Lack of Evidence for an Anti-Christian Jewish Prayer in Late Antiquity," in *Jewish and Christian Self-Definition* (ed. E. P. Sanders), 2:226–244; Steven T. Katz, "Issues in the Separation of Judaism and Christianity

after 70 c.e.: A Reconsideration," *JBL* 103 (1984) 48–53, 63–76; and
Archie L. Nations, "Jewish Persecution of Christians in the Gospel of
John," paper read at the Society of Biblical Literature annual meeting,
Atlanta, Ga., Nov. 23, 1986.

62. Kimelman's suggestion that the notion of expulsion from the
synagogue may have been "concocted" by the author of the gospel to
keep Christians away from the synagogue (*"Birkat Ha-Minim,"*
234–235) does not square with the emphasis and the emotional
coloring given the subject in its three occurrences; his claim that the
author had no knowledge of or interest in the precise identity of
Jewish leadership groups (ibid., 396 n. 53) is totally unsupported. On
the expulsion from the synagogue and its significance, cf. Wengst,
Gemeinde, 48–60; and on the role of the Pharisees, ibid., 40–44.

63. Cf. Wengst, *Gemeinde,* 58–59.

64. The frequently made suggestion that *Ioudaioi* in John should
often be understood not as a derogatory "Jews" but as a neutral
geographical designation, "Judeans," has only limited value (Wengst,
Gemeinde, 39–40). Even in John 11, where it seems most promising,
the *Ioudaioi* are hostile to Jesus (11:8) and distinct from him and his
followers; some of them believe in him—but others report on him to
the Pharisees (11:45–46). Wayne Meeks points out that Bar Kokhba,
writing in Greek, speaks of a festival "of the *Ioudaioi"* and that no
distinction between geographical and religious/ethnic use of the term
may have been made ("'Am I a Jew?'" 181–182). Even the apparent
geographical distinction between *Ioudaioi* and Galileans, whatever its
background in Johannine history, may actually function symbolically:
"Galileans" are those who accept the message of Jesus, *Ioudaioi* those
who reject it (Jouette M. Bassler, "The Galileans: A Neglected Factor
in Johannine Community Research," *CBQ* 43 [1981] 243–257).

65. Meeks, "Man from Heaven," 70; Käsemann, *Testament,* 38–40,
65–66; D. Moody Smith, "Johannine Christianity," in Smith, *Johannine Christianity,* 3–4; and Fernando Segovia, "The Love and Hatred
of Jesus and Johannine Sectarianism," *CBQ* 43 (1981) 258–272.

66. Brown, *Community,* 14–17, 88–91; cf. Barrett, *Gospel According to St. John,* 135, 139.

67. Brown, *Community,* 15, 89.

68. Bryan R. Wilson, *Magic and the Millennium: A Sociological
Study of Religious Movements of Protest Among Tribal and Third-
World Peoples.* See especially the discussion of sectarian taxonomy on
pp. 18–30.

69. Ibid., 23–24.

70. Ibid., 24.

71. Ibid., 45.

72. Its characteristics include the expectation of a supernaturally

wrought destruction and re-creation of the world's order, specifically its social order, in which believers participate, but only as assisting an already turning wheel, the essential act being that of God. "Men have no hope except from a new dispensation, and the creation of such a new order is the intention of god or the gods. . . . No subjective reorientation will affect the state of the world: its objective condition must be recognized. It will be changed only by divine action" (Wilson, *Magic and the Millennium*, 23).

73. Wilson, *Magic and the Millennium*, 22.

74. Ibid., 26, 30.

75. Thomas F. Johnson, "Sectarianism and the Johannine Community," *JBL*, forthcoming. The paper was originally read at the Society of Biblical Literature annual meeting, Atlanta, Ga., Nov. 23, 1986.

76. Robin Scroggs had earlier used seven similar features to show that the Christianity of the Synoptic traditions can be called a "sect" in this sociological sense ("The Earliest Christian Communities as Sectarian Movement," in *Christianity, Judaism and Other Greco-Roman Cults* [ed. Jacob Neusner], 2:1–23). Of these seven, it seems clear that at least four are strikingly prominent in the Johannine community as well, namely, the rejection of the establishment's view of reality, and the creation of a new reality with different assumptions; the vitality of love and mutual acceptance within the group; the voluntary nature of the group; and the demand of total commitment to the sect's new reality.

77. Martyn, "Glimpses," 107–121; and Brown, *Community,* 71–88.

78. Cf. Brown, *Community,* 93–144. Works such as those of Thyen, Segovia, and Woll mentioned above often connect these later developments to stages of the gospel's redaction. Such redaction clearly exists, particularly in the Farewell Discourses, though its relation to communal dissension seems more doubtful. Our studies will focus on areas other than the Farewell Discourses, but occasionally questions of the redaction of the gospel will arise here too, e.g., concerning John 3 and John 6.

79. As, in various ways, Fortna, *Gospel of Signs,* esp. pp. 221–234; J. Louis Martyn, "Source Criticism and Religionsgeschichte in the Fourth Gospel," in *Jesus and Man's Hope* (ed. David G. Buttrick), 1:247–273; D. Moody Smith, "The Milieu of the Johannine Miracle Source" and "The Setting and Shape of a Johannine Narrative Source," in Smith, *Johannine Christianity,* 62–79 and 80–93, respectively; Richter, "Präsentische und futurische Eschatologie"; and Thyen, "Entwicklungen."

80. See especially the works by Brown and Lindars referred to in nn. 30 and 31 above.

81. John G. Gager, "Social Description and Social Explanation in the Study of Early Christianity: A Review Essay," in *The Bible and Liberation* (ed. Gottwald), 429; and Scroggs, "The Sociological Interpretation of the New Testament," in *The Bible and Liberation* (ed. Gottwald), 341.

82. Bruce J. Malina, *The Gospel of John in Sociolinguistic Perspective,* came into my hands only after the manuscript of this book was completed. Applying a variety of sociological models to John, Malina arrives at a number of conclusions with which I would be fully in accord, e.g., that for the Johannine community "previous lines defining and delimiting meaningful social relations and institutions are largely eradicated" (p. 11) and that Johannine language is an "antilanguage" produced by a group set up as a conscious alternative to a larger society (pp. 11–17). It seems to me, however, that Malina (like more traditional interpreters) greatly overestimates John's individualism. As we shall see, there is a considerable concern in John for group adherence and group solidarity; Johannine faith is by no means purely a matter of individual relationship to Jesus.

2

Nicodemus and the Blind Man: Choices of Faith and Community

Several of our studies will concern Nicodemus, the Pharisee who comes to Jesus by night in John 3 and is engaged by him in a dialogue about the kingdom of God and the Son of Man. This may be somewhat surprising, given the seemingly minor part Nicodemus plays in the gospel as a whole. Yet Nicodemus appears as often as any other of the "minor characters" in John, and always in a significant role in relation to Jesus. Considering that (unlike, say, John the Baptist or Pontius Pilate) he is otherwise unknown in early Christian tradition, this persistent appearance suggests that he may have had some special significance for the Fourth Evangelist and his community. As we will see, he seems in fact to symbolize an important element in the Johannine milieu, and it will be good for us to devote some time to exploring his role in general before we look at its implications for particular aspects of John's thought. Balanced against Nicodemus is the blind man of John 9, who is healed by Jesus and then brought before the Pharisees. He too is a powerfully symbolic figure, whose story can help us understand much about how the Johannine community interpreted its experience, particularly in contrast to the people represented by Nicodemus. We will therefore begin by studying just these two contrasting figures.

Nicodemus

As the foregoing discussion suggests, my focus will not be on Nicodemus as a historical person but rather on the symbolic role he plays in the Fourth Gospel. That there was at least one prominent man named Nicodemus living in Jerusalem prior to the First Revolt is known from Jewish sources, but their information sheds no light on the figure in John 3.[1] All that we know about John's Nicodemus is what John tells us, and as usual he seems less concerned with the meaning of this character for Jesus' history than with his meaning for the history of the Johannine community.[2]

If Nicodemus is a symbolic figure in John, what does he symbolize? He is usually seen as a man who was genuinely interested in Jesus but failed to understand him, and only later came to something like faith in him. In the dialogue in John 3, Nicodemus remains uncomprehending of his need for a spiritual rebirth from God, so that Rudolf Bultmann, for example, saw in him "man as he is," in need of an entirely new origin for his salvation and yet unable to see the possibility of it.[3]

In this view, Nicodemus' need, and the transformation that is offered to him, is essentially an inner and individual one. Recent developments in Johannine studies, however, have opened up the possibility of seeing something more than this in Nicodemus: we can now see the role that he plays as a *communal* symbolic figure.

According to John 2:23–25, Jesus did not trust himself to certain people in Jerusalem who had believed in him when they saw the signs that he did, because "he knew what was in a man." When Nicodemus is then immediately introduced as "a man," who, moreover, regards Jesus as a teacher come from God because of the signs that he does, he is clearly meant to portray one of these untrustworthy believers.[4] Furthermore, he speaks to Jesus in the plural, and Jesus likewise addresses him in the plural. Nicodemus says, not "I know," but *"We know that you are a teacher come from God"* (3:2), and Jesus subsequently tells him, *"You people must be born again"* (3:7). Indeed, Jesus applies the plural both to himself and to Nicodemus when he says, *"We speak of what we know, and testify to what we have seen, and you people do not accept our testimony"*; and then refers to his speaking to *"you people"* of earthly and heavenly things, which *"you people"* fail to believe (3:11–12).[5] Since the interview is represented as taking place alone at night, these plurals are both surprising and significant. Nicodemus evidently does not stand for himself alone but for some specific group, which is rather negatively portrayed. In the same manner Jesus undoubtedly speaks for the Johannine Christians and stands for them here over against the group represented by Nicodemus.[6]

Nicodemus is identified in 3:1 as a Pharisee and a "ruler of the Jews." Although he acknowledges Jesus as a teacher, in 3:10 Jesus ironically calls *him* "the teacher of Israel" and seems astonished at his lack of understanding. It may be that Nicodemus' own claim to be Israel's teacher is part of what interferes with his ability to grasp and acknowledge the claim of Jesus. In addressing Jesus as "teacher,"

Nicodemus essentially seeks to place him on the same level with himself, something that would be quite unacceptable from the Johannine point of view. We may say at this point, then, that Nicodemus is pictured as a Pharisee, one in a position of authority, who acknowledges the miracles of Jesus but cannot reach real faith in him while he retains his own claim to be Israel's teacher. It would seem plausible that the group he symbolizes might also be characterized in this way.

This impression is confirmed at Nicodemus' next appearance, in John 7:45–52. Here the Pharisees' own officers, sent out to arrest Jesus, return awed by him instead. They are rebuked with the rhetorical question whether anyone "of the rulers or of the Pharisees" has believed in Jesus; and those who do believe are vilified as a "mob that does not know the law," who are "under a curse." But at this point Nicodemus speaks up, Nicodemus who has been described as a Pharisee and a ruler and who is pointedly identified here again as "one of them." Now would be his chance to prove the other Pharisees wrong, and to defend the ignorant rabble they have scorned, by confessing his own faith in Jesus. But does he do so? He asks, "Does our law condemn a man unless it first hears from him and finds out what he does?" Some would hold that these words, containing an indirect defense of Jesus, are therefore an implicit testimony to Nicodemus' faith.[7] But it is hardly likely that this timid legal quibble would constitute a confession of faith satisfactory to the Fourth Evangelist. On the contrary, though it properly disputes the legality of Jesus' condemnation, Nicodemus' reply remains confined to the realm of Pharisaic legal debate.[8] It is significant that Nicodemus speaks of "our law," for in John the law is always the law of the Jews or of Moses, never of Jesus or of his disciples.[9] Nicodemus thus remains the would-be "teacher of Israel" who cannot bring himself to a real confession of faith in Jesus.[10]

In fact, his case is exactly that of the "rulers" mentioned in John 12:42–43, who believed in Jesus but would not confess for fear that the Pharisees would put them out of the synagogue. Here the rulers *(archontes)* and the Pharisees form two distinct and even opposing groups, which has led one scholar to suggest that by "rulers" John always refers to secret believers among the Jewish authorities, in contrast to the hostile Pharisees.[11] Yet in Nicodemus the two groups are clearly united (3:1; 7:50c), so that even the Pharisees do not appear as a monolithic body (as can be seen also in 9:16), and we must reckon with covert Christians even among them. John's opinion of these believers is not good: they prefer the glory that comes from human beings to that which comes from God (12:43); and it would seem that Nicodemus must be ranked among them.[12]

Nicodemus last appears in John 19:38–42, where (brought in, no doubt, by John himself)[13] he accompanies Joseph of Arimathea in the burial of Jesus. Note that John characterizes Joseph as a disciple who concealed his discipleship for fear of the Jews, thus bending the common tradition about him (cf. Mark 15:43; Matt. 27:57) so as to align him too with the fearful believing rulers of 12:42–43. Nicodemus' contribution here is to bring no less than seventy-five pounds of burial spices, a gesture often seen as one of true and open devotion, even of confession.[14] It is more likely an act of unbelief.[15] Alfred Loisy pointed out long ago that Nicodemus and Joseph confess nothing and have nothing to do with Jesus except with his corpse.[16] Nicodemus shows himself capable only of burying Jesus, ponderously and with a kind of absurd finality, so loading him down with burial as to make it clear that Nicodemus does not expect a resurrection any more than he expects a second birth.[17]

Throughout the gospel, then, Nicodemus appears as a man of inadequate faith and inadequate courage, and as such he represents a *group* that the author wishes to characterize in this way. Evidently members of this group may hold positions of authority, may even be Pharisees themselves, but their status makes them fearful rather than bold in confessing their faith in Jesus. Moreover, even the faith they have apparently falls short of Johannine standards. Nicodemus sees in Jesus no more than a teacher, and even then fails totally to comprehend his teaching. Jesus tells him, "We speak of what we know and testify to what we have seen, and you people do not accept our testimony" (3:11). Shortly after this, there follows the claim that the Son of Man has not only gone up into heaven but come down from there as well. It was this claim that the Nicodemus Christians were unwilling to admit, this "testimony" that they refused to accept. The christological issue was clearly a major dividing line, for as Marinus de Jonge stresses, their inadequate Christology leaves them, in John's view, outside the true believing community.[18]

This group, symbolized by Nicodemus, was one that was present in the environment of the Johannine community. It was the group that J. Louis Martyn and Raymond Brown have described as secret Christian Jews, or "crypto-Christians" (although Brown does not regard Nicodemus as a representative of this group).[19] Its members were prepared to acknowledge Jesus as having been a divinely sent teacher and miracle worker, perhaps as standing in the line of the prophets, if Martyn's analysis of John 8:53 is correct; but no more than this. The characterization of Nicodemus in John 3 and 7 suggests that even some Pharisaic teaching authorities were included among their number, though we need not think that all were so highly placed. Apparently they hoped to be disciples of Jesus but also to remain within the framework of synagogue Judaism. In the Johannine situation, this could only be done by concealing their discipleship from public knowledge, avoiding an open confession, for it is clear that known Christians were being expelled from the synagogue. The full dimensions of their Christianity, how they managed their concealment, and what mechanism if any there was for exposing them we do not know.[20] Apparently they were successful enough at avoiding detection to have caused considerable distress to John and his community.

We will have more to say about this group and the relationship of the Johannine community to them in the course of our further studies. They will figure so largely because it seems evident that they figured largely in the experience and the thinking of the Johannine group. Both their inadequate Christology and their fear of being known draw down harsh criticism from the Fourth Evangelist. Yet there is a note of poignancy too, especially in Nicodemus' failure to defend the unlettered believers in 7:45–52, as if the evangelist were appealing to this group even now to reveal themselves and openly to join—and help—the new Christian community. Indeed, it may well be that if the Fourth Gospel has a missionary intent toward anyone, it is toward these secret believers.

The Blind Man in John 9

As Brown observes, the blind man whose story is told in John 9 "is acting out the history of the Johannine community," refusing to take the way of concealment followed by the crypto-Christians.[21] It is for this reason that I have chosen to examine his portrayal in conjunction with that of Nicodemus.

In his path-breaking study of how Johannine communal history is depicted in the Fourth Gospel, Martyn used the story of the blind man as his parade example.[22] Placed at the climax of Jesus' debates with "the Jews," this story sums up in a remarkably lucid and compact way what the Fourth Evangelist had to say about his community's relationship to Jesus, to the synagogue authorities, and to the secret believers. It is a symbolic story in the best sense, not an allegory, for the actions and words of its characters remain for the most part quite natural and unforced, but a representation in memorably vivid narrative form of the events and convictions that molded the Johannine community and the Fourth Gospel itself.

The story and much of what can be said about it are well known,[23] and we may begin with a rapid overview before examining a few items in more detail. At the beginning of the chapter Jesus and his disciples encounter a blind man in the streets of Jerusalem. The disciples

inquire whose sin is responsible for the man's blindness; Jesus, after a
brief reply concerning sin and the works of God, proceeds with the
healing. The man's acquaintances ask in astonishment about his cure,
which he describes, and his healer, whose whereabouts he does not
know. He is then haled before the Pharisees, since the healing took
place on a sabbath, again describes how he was healed, and causes a
division among the Pharisees as to whether Jesus is from God or a
sinner. He himself declares Jesus to be a prophet. Then his parents are
questioned; they acknowledge that their son was born blind but are
unwilling to discuss his recovery, since "the Jews" have decreed that
anyone who confesses Jesus to be the Messiah is to be expelled from
the synagogue. The blind man himself is now recalled but refuses to
tell his story again. At the end of an acrimonious discussion, he
informs the Pharisees that Jesus must be from God or he could not
have healed him, and the Pharisees throw him out. Jesus then comes
looking for him and receives from him a confession of faith in himself
as the Son of Man. At the conclusion, Jesus declares that he has come
to heal the blind and to blind those who see; when the Pharisees take
offense, Jesus says that their sin consists not in their blindness but in
their claim to see.

Not least among this story's remarkable features is the fact that
Jesus himself is absent from it for twenty-seven of its forty-one verses,
much longer than any other span in the gospel. For events to be told
without Jesus being in them, they must surely have great significance
for John in their own right. The blind man, it seems clear, symbolizes
the Johannine Christians. They have received their sight, as he does,
from the one who is the Light of the World, and they have suffered, as
he does, for their confession of it. His conduct no doubt stands not
only for what has been done but for what should be done under such
circumstances. His attitude before the Pharisees is daring to the point
of insolence, in obvious contrast to the behavior of his own parents
and that of Nicodemus in 7:50–51. Indeed, its nearest parallel is Jesus'
demeanor before the high priest in 18:19–23. Perhaps this very
parallel explains why Jesus can be absent from the central episodes of
the story: his role is taken over by the blind man himself. The blind
man, then, represents what is both possible and necessary, for the
individual and for the community, when facing the synagogue authorities.

These authorities are of course symbolized by the Pharisees of the
story. They possess full official power over the Jewish community—
indeed, "the Pharisees" (9:13, 15, 16) are interchangeable with "the
Jews" (9:18, 22). Such a role for the Pharisees, like the threat of
excommunication with which it is connected, would be quite anachro-
nistic in the context of Jesus' lifetime but no doubt represents the

actual state of affairs, at least locally, at the time of the gospel's writing.[24] Why the Pharisees are so implacably hostile to the disciples of "that man" is not made clear, and indeed we know relatively little about the motivation for the persecution that the Johannine community experienced. Theological aversion to the developing Johannine Christology is the most obvious and most likely suggestion, but one could equally well speculate on fear of pollution from the Christians' freer relationships with Gentiles, a desire to strengthen communal cohesion in the aftermath of the First Revolt, or even a simple rivalry for power, as contributing factors. It is clear, at any rate, that the Pharisaic authorities in the community's locale were determined that Christianity should not gain a sizable following there and were taking steps to prevent it.

Yet it is interesting to note that the Pharisees themselves suffer a schism over Jesus as a result of the blind man's first testimony. Some say he cannot be from God because he violates the sabbath; others question how a sinner could do such signs: "So there was a division among them" (9:16). This may be meant to signify the presence of Nicodemus-style secret believers among the authorities (cf. 3:2). But either the rift is healed by the time the blind man is called before them again, when the Pharisees speak as one, or else their unanimous avowal that they are disciples of Moses, not of Jesus (9:28–29), is meant to imply that those sympathetic to the Christians are not only concealing their sympathy but actually taking part in the persecution.[25] The blind man's parents represent the secret believers even more clearly still, this time among the common people, afraid even to acknowledge the miracles of Jesus for fear they will be expelled from the synagogue.

This gives us a general idea of the meaning of the story for John and his readers. It remains to examine in more detail the blind man's progressive acknowledgment of Jesus and the curious role played by his parents. But first we must look at another theme which can be found running right through the narrative yet which has seldom been given the attention it deserves.

"Rabbi, who sinned, this man or his parents, that he was born blind?" This question from the disciples at the beginning of the story is an extremely discomforting one, and the discomfort is not greatly eased by commentators' references to ancient ideas about the punishment of children for their parents' sins, prenatal sin, or even the preexistence of souls. It would help somewhat if we could see the question as ironic, demonstrating by the example of congenital blindness the absurdity of such explanations for human suffering.[26] Yet Jesus' reply seems to take the question seriously: "Neither this man nor his parents sinned, but that the works of God might be made manifest in him." Despite a hopeful beginning, as theodicy this is really worse yet. It seems to say that God did not even blind the man for his entire lifetime in order to punish some wrongdoing; he did it merely to show off his own power by finally sending Jesus around to heal him. Perhaps our age is simply too sensitive to the rights of individuals and the wrongness of undeserved suffering; but few of us will find such a teaching tolerable.

I do not think, however, that this is in fact what the passage means. Theodicy here is the disciples' interest, and Jesus' answer says that it is the wrong one. Grammatically, he changes the man's blindness from a result to a cause. The disciples' question, and the viewpoint behind it, are rejected altogether. They see suffering as an occasion for moralizing about the victim. Jesus sees it as an occasion for doing the works of God, that is, for relieving the suffering.[27] John refuses the question of technical theodicy and points instead to the need that the works of God should be "made manifest," that they should appear, and therefore that what they are should also appear. The "work of God," it turns out, is not punishing sinners with suffering but overcoming the suffering. If, as is widely recognized, the man's blindness symbolizes the world's "darkness," into which Jesus comes as healing light,[28] this brief dialogue may also signify John's lack of interest in cosmological speculation about how the darkness came about. Simply, the world *is* blind, and it is God's work to heal it.

But the question "Who sinned?" is not laid to rest with this. Rather, it recurs again and again as a theme underlying the entire story. Verbs and nouns relating to sin occur in a higher concentration in this chapter than anywhere else in John. The disciples suggest that either the blind man or his parents must have sinned (9:2). Jesus says that neither of them sinned (v. 3). Some of the Pharisees assert that Jesus is a sinner (v. 16); others deny this, but later they all emphatically affirm that he is a sinner (v. 24). The blind man replies that Jesus cannot be a sinner (vs. 25, 31–33). The Pharisees respond by reverting, ironically enough, to the disciples' position and declaring that the blind man was born in sin (v. 34). But in the end Jesus avows that it is the Pharisees themselves whose sin remains (v. 41).[29] Thus the entirety of John 9 is dominated by the question "Who is a sinner?"

The first way of answering this question, as we have seen, is through the common idea of divine punishment: the man is blind, so someone must have sinned. This is the disciples' answer, and evidently the Pharisees also take it up in 9:34.[30] But it is dismissed by Jesus as the wrong approach to the problem at the very beginning of the story. A much more serious answer, in its intent and in its possible consequences for the Johannine community, is the one with which the Pharisees primarily concern themselves. "We know that this man"—

Jesus—"is a sinner," they avow in 9:24. How do they know it? According to 9:16, the test is the keeping of the sabbath. Jesus does not do so, and therefore he is a sinner. In other words, the Pharisees appeal to the well-known standard of God's revelation, the law of Moses, universally accepted as normative, even if interpretations of it may differ. This norm provides an obvious criterion by which it may be judged who is a sinner and who is not. "We know that God has spoken to Moses, but as for this fellow, we do not know where he comes from" (9:29).

John 9:16, however, also suggests the existence of another test, applied, at first at any rate, by some of the Pharisees: "How can a sinful man do such signs?" It is not they, however, but the blind man who takes this up and develops it, in the pivotal sentence of the chapter: "Whether he is a sinner I do not know; I know only one thing, that though I was blind, I now see" (9:25). Here the blind man sets the one thing he is certain of, his own experience, against the standards with which the Pharisees confront him. If it comes down to a clash between what has happened to him and what, according to the rules, can or cannot possibly happen, he has no choice but to assent to the reality he now knows. The blind man's God does not live in a book, not even the book of the law itself, but in the act of mercy that has been done to him. He is not about to give up this act, or the freedom of his God to commit it, even for the sake of Moses. "We know that God does not listen to sinners," he declares. "If this man were not from God, he could do nothing" (9:31, 33).

In this we may feel quite certain that he reflects the position of the Johannine community. They also have felt themselves enlightened by him whom the Pharisees, for the most part, regard as a sinner. They must either suppress their own experience or stand by it in defiance of those who, in their society, are in charge of communal norms and their interpretation. Johannine Christianity is thus not merely a subculture but a counterculture within at least the local Judaism wherein it has precipitated so painful a conflict. The Johannine Christians have experienced God anew in Jesus, and from their perspective to be told that their confession of Jesus is illegitimate is to be told that they must confine their experience of reality itself to what the ruling authorities define as acceptable. This they cannot do. To retreat from their allegiance to Jesus would be like saying that their experience has in fact been nothing at all; and how can that be possible? "Once I was blind, but now I can see!"

The progressive nature of the blind man's coming to christological understanding and confession has often been observed. At first he knows the one who healed him only as "the man called Jesus" (9:11). Later, before the Pharisees, he acknowledges Jesus as a prophet (v. 17) and then, more strongly, as having come from God (v. 33). Finally, confronted by Jesus himself, he worships him as Son of Man (vs. 35–38).[31] This pattern is found elsewhere in John as well—for example, with the Samaritan woman in John 4. It signifies the supreme importance for the Fourth Evangelist of coming to correct faith in Jesus. Simply to acknowledge him as a divinely inspired teacher or prophet, or in other merely human ways, is not enough. It is necessary to reach the full Johannine christological confession, and hence the gospel culminates in the words of "doubting" Thomas, whose doubts are dissolved in the confession "My Lord and my God" (20:28).

What is especially significant about the blind man's progressive christological enlightenment is the circumstances under which it develops. He reaches deeper understanding, not in a reflective encounter with Jesus, as Thomas and the Samaritan woman do, but in the process of *confrontation* with the Pharisees. Once again this may represent the Fourth Evangelist's interpretation of the history of his own community. They have come to know the Son of Man by starting from an awareness of having been "healed" by him and then stubbornly championing this against an opposition based on given norms rather than on living experience. The blind man's understanding of who Jesus is emerges from his struggle with those who would invalidate the experience of his own life. And this is the model that John holds up to his community: let what has happened to you bring you into conflict with the rulers, with Moses himself if need be; for in this *process* your enlightenment will be completed, and at its end you will meet the one who granted you your sight and know him for who he is.

It is important to grasp this aspect of the Fourth Gospel. John's christological absolutism could easily appear to be simply a demand for conformity to a foreordained dogma, at the price of one's salvation. But in fact that demand is what is caricatured in the Pharisees in this story. Johannine Christology initiated, but also developed out of, a life-and-death conflict with the synagogue authorities. It was not thought out in a study or decreed in a council, though one cannot deny the thinking that must have gone into it. Once it had even begun to be conceived, it had to be struggled for, and the struggle itself was the matrix for its refinement and completion. The blind man's story is the image of that struggle and its consummation, so far as the Fourth Evangelist could yet see it. It tells us that, for the Johannine community, the truth about Jesus came, not at the beginning, nor even simply at the end, but out of the midst of this process of confession, rebuke, and stubbornly continued confession itself. The story's point was that people faced with the blind man's choice should follow the blind man's course, confident that even expulsion from the synagogue would mean, not catastrophe, but a deepened encounter with the one who had given them sight.

This exhortation climaxes in Jesus' concluding words in 9:39–41. Here he declares that he came into the world for judgment, that the blind might see and the seeing become blind. The Pharisees characteristically misunderstand and ask if he is accusing them of blindness. This allows him the final stroke: "If you were blind, you would have no sin. But as it is, you say, 'We see': so your sin remains." The collocation of blindness and sin forms an inclusion with the opening verses of John 9. The question of who is a sinner has now come full circle, and the import of vs. 2–4 is further underlined. By the conventional standards, both Jesus and the blind man are sinners. The latter's healing really begins in v. 3, where Jesus refuses to regard him as a sinner and carries out the compassionate work of God toward him. It culminates in his final confession of Jesus, wherein he himself denies, and defies, the Pharisees' definition of them both as sinners. Its ultimate ratification comes here at the end of the story. Jesus, we are reminded, has come not to explain blindness but to do away with it. It is no sin to be blind; sin comes in rejecting the work of God, and it is this sin which, at the coming of Jesus, blinds those who claim to see. So it is not the Pharisees in their piety and their authority who see what is most important to see, but a blind beggar, who sees more and more even as he takes his stand against them.

Before we leave this story, we need to look at one other somewhat neglected feature of it, the action of the blind man's parents (9:18–23). Their frightened babbling when the Pharisees question them about their son's condition and his healing is almost comic: "We know that this is our son and that he was born blind, but how it is that he now sees we don't know, or who opened his eyes, we don't know—ask him, he is of age, he'll speak for himself!" Almost comic, but not quite. It is remarkable that commentators regularly take note of the parents' motivation—they were, as John explains, afraid of "the Jews," who had decreed expulsion from the synagogue for anyone who confessed Jesus to be the Messiah—but not of what it is that they do. Observe that it is not their protestations of ignorance to which John draws attention; rather, he emphasizes that in their fear they said, "He is of age, ask him" (v. 23). The terrible perfidy of this remark is perhaps the most shocking thing in the entire story. The parents have not only tried to shield themselves from scrutiny, they have deliberately turned the inquisitors' attention back upon their own son, knowing full well that he will be subject to the very sentence that they themselves are afraid to face.

To what extent their behavior reflects actual events in the history of the Johannine community is, of course, impossible to know.[32] The parents' chief function here is to serve as a foil to the courage of their son. As symbols of the secret Christians, they present an even more negative image than Nicodemus. They remind the reader that, in the Johannine situation, to avoid an open confession had implications not only for the believer fearful of exposure but also for the others who took the risk and allowed themselves to be involved in the process of confrontation. Self-protection entails the betrayal of others; every individual act has communal consequences. The blind man and his parents are both faced with a choice in John 9, and their responses to it could not be more sharply differentiated. The original question asked by the disciples thus receives an unexpectedly ironic answer. "Who sinned, the blind man or his parents?" Neither of them sinned to cause his blindness; but as a result of his healing, the blind man steps fully into the light, while his parents are found to remain in sin after all.

Conclusions

Nicodemus and the blind man are "historical" figures in the gospel of John, not in the sense of their being figures from the past in whom the gospel writer is interested, but as representatives of historical realities in the experience of the Johannine community. The exercise of a modest amount of historical imagination affords us, through them, an insight into both the complexity and the strain of the situation confronting that community. There are choices to be made: to believe or to disbelieve, to join one party or the other, to speak or to remain silent. On one side stand the Pharisees, now taking the role of guardians of the Jewish community's traditional faith and values, and doing so in a time, following the catastrophe of the First Revolt, of great stress for that community. On the other side stand the Johannine Christians, with their undeniable courage and their radical claims about Jesus of Nazareth and what is offered by God in him. In the middle stand Nicodemus and Joseph of Arimathea, the blind man and his parents, people of high rank and low who have been moved by this message and who, if they have given their assent to it, may feel themselves transformed, given new sight, by it. It is noteworthy that of the several symbolic figures we have studied in this chapter, it is not the highly placed Nicodemus or Joseph but the blind beggar who acts most strongly and most successfully, from the evangelist's point of view, when the decision is before him. The Pharisees' contempt for the blind man, expressed in their dismissal of him as "born entirely in sin" (9:34), applies not only to him in his affliction but to the Johannine Christians generally, in the same manner as the disparage-

ment of the "rabble" in 7:49. It is to be linked, perhaps, to the early
Pharisaic disdain for the *'am ha-aretz,* the people of lesser learning
and piety, and of suspect faithfulness to the law, contact with whom
was, for purity's sake, largely avoided. It may be that the Johannine
Christians included a considerable contingent of such people; at any
rate, the Pharisees among them were obviously very few indeed. The
selection of the beggar to serve as the positive role model, and the
audacity and strength of character with which he is endowed, certainly
suggest that John felt no obligation to curry favor with the dominant
religious and social powers.

The portraits we have examined also suggest the sharp sense of
betrayal felt by the confessing members of the Johannine group at the
reluctance of those who hung back. Whether this sense, and these
portraits, are justified or not is, of course, an open question. Raymond
Brown may be right in suggesting that from the crypto-Christians'
point of view the blind man would have been an "insolent enthusiast,"
and the Johannine Christians would have been burning bridges that
did not yet need to be burned.[33] It is not an easy judgment for an
outsider to make, and we are outsiders to that first-century situation.
Nonetheless, some of the most powerful theological statements in the
Fourth Gospel are intimately linked to that ancient and many-sided
conflict, and if we are to interpret them reliably we must not neglect
their true context. Our further studies will attempt to take this context
into account in examining several well-known literary and theological
questions in John.

NOTES

1. See, e.g., Barrett, *Gospel According to St. John,* 204; Brown,
Gospel According to John, 1:129–130; and Lindars, *Gospel of John,*
149.

2. "Like all John's characters, he has a symbolical function,
whether he is an historical person or not" (Lindars, *Gospel of John*).

3. Bultmann, *Gospel of John,* 133–143. Bultmann also speaks of
Nicodemus as representing the inadequacy of specifically Jewish
questions and answers (ibid., 134, 144).

4. Bultmann (*Gospel of John,* 133) and Schnackenburg (*Gospel
According to St John,* 1:365) deny this; Loisy (*Quatrième évangile,*
304), Brown (*Gospel According to John,* 1:135), and others affirm it.

5. For the sake of clarity I have slightly overtranslated the Greek
second person plural forms as "you people" instead of simply "you."
The Revised Standard Version misses this nuance; it is caught by the

New International Version, and partly by the New English Bible and the Jerusalem Bible—and, of course, by the distinction in the King James Version between "thee" and "ye."

6. Cf. Barrett, *Gospel According to St. John,* 211.

7. E.g., Bultmann, *Gospel of John,* 311; and Brown, *Gospel According to John,* 1:330.

8. Cf. Marinus de Jonge, "Nicodemus and Jesus: Some Observations on Misunderstanding and Understanding in the Fourth Gospel," in de Jonge, *Jesus,* 34–36.

9. The law of Moses, of course, bears witness to Jesus (John 5:39–40, 45–47; Nicodemus, however, does not speak of this); and Jesus can appeal to "your law" to make a point (7:19–24; 8:17; 10:34). Yet it always remains *"their* law" (15:25; cf. 18:31; 19:7), in contrast to the grace and truth imparted to believers through Jesus Christ (1:14, 17).

10. Barrett, *Gospel According to St. John,* 332. R. Alan Culpepper's study of Nicodemus *(Anatomy of the Fourth Gospel: A Study in Literary Design,* 134–136) likewise concludes that he remains "one of them."

11. Martyn, *History and Theology,* 87–88.

12. So also Wengst, *Gemeinde,* 59–60.

13. Schnackenburg, *Gospel According to St John,* 3:295; and Lindars, *Gospel of John,* 592.

14. Brown, *Gospel According to John,* 2:959–960; idem, *Community,* 72 n. 128; Schnackenburg, *Gospel According to St John,* 3:296–297; and Lindars, *Gospel of John,* 592.

15. Cf. Meeks, "Man from Heaven," 55; de Jonge, "Nicodemus and Jesus," in de Jonge, *Jesus,* 33–34; and Duke, *Irony,* 110.

16. Loisy, *Quatrième évangile,* 895–896.

17. One is tempted to say that Nicodemus, like Caesar's Antony but without his irony, has come to bury Jesus, not to raise him.

18. De Jonge, "Nicodemus and Jesus," in de Jonge, *Jesus,* 30–32, 37–42. Jürgen Becker ("J 3, 1–21 als Reflex johanneischer Schuldiskussion," in *Das Wort und die Wörter,* ed. Horst Balz and Siegfried Schulz, 86–88) finds that Nicodemus represents a group of quasi-Jewish Christian teachers with a false Christology, opposed by the group represented by Jesus.

19. Martyn, "Glimpses," 109–115; and Brown, *Community,* 71–73. Martyn makes no explicit reference to Nicodemus, but cf. his *History and Theology,* 87–88. Cf. already Loisy, *Quatrième évangile,* 305.

20. See the discussion of the Benediction against Heretics in chapter 1 above.

21. Brown, *Community,* 72.

22. Martyn, *History and Theology,* 24–62.

23. See the commentaries, e.g., Brown, *Gospel According to John,* 1:369–382; and Schnackenburg, *Gospel According to St John,* 2:238–258.

24. Cf. Wengst, *Gemeinde,* 42–44, 49–50.

25. Note the possibility that secret Christians even collaborated in the martyrdom of Johannine believers, raised in connection with John 8:31–59 by Martyn ("Glimpses," 114); also his discussion of the expression "disciples of Moses" (ibid., 108–109). Conceivably the Pharisees "who were with him" whom Jesus condemns in 9:40–41 are also meant to refer to such believers; but the words may imply no more than accidental physical proximity (Schnackenburg, *Gospel According to St John,* 2:256, with n. 57).

26. Cf. Bultmann, *Gospel of John,* 330 n. 8.

27. Cf. Archibald M. Hunter, *The Gospel According to John,* 95.

28. So, e.g., Dodd, *Interpretation,* 357.

29. Once again several contemporary translations obscure the theme by translating *hamartia* as "guilt" rather than "sin" in this climactic occurrence.

30. So, e.g., Bultmann, *Gospel of John,* 337; and Barrett, *Gospel According to St. John,* 364.

31. See, e.g., Brown, *Gospel According to John,* 1:377; and Schnackenburg, *Gospel According to St John,* 2:239, both of whom also note the correspondingly regressive statements of the Pharisees.

The authenticity of 9:38, the blind man's worship of Jesus, is in some doubt, being omitted by the important manuscripts P[75], Sinaiticus, and W. On the one hand it seems much more likely that such a verse would be deliberately added by later copyists than deliberately omitted, suggesting that these manuscripts have the original reading. On the other hand, though the blind man's response could be inferred from 9:36, this sentence seems an almost necessary conclusion to his story; and we may note the surely false readings of P[75] and Sinaiticus in 8:57 ("seen you") and 9:4 ("sent us").

32. The whole subject of intergenerational conflict as a feature in the rise of early Christianity would seem to be well worth investigating. Mark 13:12 may not be merely a stereotyped apocalyptic prediction of final woes. Also, it is interesting to note that the Lukan parallel to it (Luke 21:16) omits children betraying their parents, and that Luke 12:53, in contrast to Matt. 10:35, adds the division of parent against child to that of child against parent from Micah 7:6.

33. Brown, *Community,* 73.

3
The Unity of John 3
as Communal Appeal

The third chapter of John has long presented exegetes with an unusually large number of problems. It seems to begin straightforwardly enough: following the cleansing of the Temple, Nicodemus comes to express his regard for Jesus. But the dialogue that follows is curiously inconsequential, as Nicodemus is first puzzled by Jesus' insistence on another birth and then rebuffed for his lack of faith. Eventually the dialogue becomes a monologue by Jesus and then trails off into a discourse on the salvation and the judgment that result from the coming of God's Son into the world. Next the scene shifts to the baptismal activity of Jesus and John the Baptist, apparently near the River Jordan. After a somewhat obscure introduction, we find another dialogue, this time between John the Baptist and his disciples regarding his own status relative to that of Jesus. But this too becomes a monologue by the Baptist and trails off into a series of pronouncements about the superiority of the one who comes from above and the necessity of believing in him.

John 3 is thus marked by a series of obscurities and difficult transitions. Why does Nicodemus come to Jesus, and why does Jesus answer him as he does? What is meant by the other birth, and what has it to do with the coming of the Son? Does Jesus' speech to Nicodemus end at some point and the evangelist's own observations begin? Why is it remarked that Jesus baptized people, and what exactly is the occasion of John the Baptist's dialogue with his disciples? Is the latter supposed to be related somehow to Jesus' dialogue with Nicodemus? Does John's speech also give way to comments by the evangelist, and if so, at what point?

Moreover, there are striking similarities between Jesus' words to Nicodemus and the words that conclude (or follow) the speech of John the Baptist in 3:31–36.[1] Both passages speak of one who comes down from heaven, of the contrast between heaven and earth, and of a testimony that is rejected. Both speak of God sending the Son, of the eternal life that believers in him receive, and of the different fate of those who disbelieve. What significance do these parallels, which follow in the same sequence in both passages, have for understanding the structure of the chapter and the relation of John the Baptist's speech to that of Jesus?

We already began to address the issues concerning Nicodemus in chapter 2; of the other questions, not all can be dealt with in detail here. What we will do is to focus first on the figures of Nicodemus and John the Baptist and then on the motif of birth from water and spirit in order to try to discover a unifying theme for John 3. This thematic unity should then in its turn shed light on the questions of compositional unity and structure that are raised by the difficulties mentioned above.

A number of solutions to the problem of John 3 have of course already been proposed. Many scholars regard the final vs. 31–36 as unsatisfactory in their present location. Rudolf Bultmann thought it most likely that they originally belonged after v. 21, as the conclusion to the speech of Jesus which they so closely resemble. The intervening vs. 22–30 would then be viewed as an appendix.[2] Rudolf Schnackenburg goes farther yet. For him, the dialogue with Nicodemus ends at v. 12, Jesus' rebuff of Nicodemus' unbelief. Originally vs. 22–30, on Jesus and John the Baptist, followed immediately. But the evangelist had also composed a "kerygmatic discourse" summarizing the message of Jesus, the present vs. 31–36 followed by vs. 13–21. This discourse was then inserted redactionally by the evangelist's disciples, in a mistaken order.[3] Raymond Brown regards 3:31–36 as an independent variant of Jesus' words in 3:11–21 (paralleled also in 12:44–50), originating with the evangelist but attached by a redactor to the end of the chapter as an interpretation of it.[4] We may note that all of these thus see vs. 31–36 as words of *Jesus* in the evangelist's intention, secondarily and wrongly given the appearance of being ascribed to John the Baptist. In a slightly different manner, Jürgen Becker sees 3:1–21 as a unity, a series of exegeses of the traditional saying in 3:3 resulting from discussions within the Johannine "school." John 3:31–36 is an additional commentary on the dialogue, placed in this somewhat unfortunate location by a copyist.[5]

Barnabas Lindars, by contrast, sees these verses as a unit related to vs. 16–21 but self-contained and deliberately held over by the evangelist himself to follow the testimony of the Baptist.[6] Other commentators too, such as C. K. Barrett and Ernst Haenchen, are willing to interpret the text in its present order.[7] Certainly this would be the most economical approach, and the simplest in regard to the history of the text's composition, if we could discover the unifying and ordering factors that would justify treating this arrangement, with all its apparent difficulties, as the evangelist's original intention.

C. H. Dodd sought this unity of the chapter in the idea of initiation or rebirth into eternal life, with the Christian baptism of water and spirit being contrasted with John's baptism of water only. Verses 31–36 then appropriately follow this contrast as a recapitulation, not a direct continuation, of the earlier passage.[8] I believe that this is in essence the correct solution; yet it does not fully account for the *joining* of the Nicodemus and John the Baptist dialogues, nor for all the nuances that follow therefrom. For vs. 22–36 are not merely an "explanatory appendix" to the preceding dialogue and discourse[9] but stand on an equal level with them. Similarly, Wayne Meeks regards 3:31–36 as a summary of the themes of the dialogue with Nicodemus, preceded by the material on the Baptist in order to emphasize the distinction between his movement and that of Jesus.[10] More recently, Jeffrey Wilson has sought to develop Dodd's insight by observing a series of structural parallels between the first and second halves of the chapter. Wilson holds that the second half is meant to reaffirm Jesus' testimony to himself out of the mouth of John the Baptist, in order to press the claims of Jesus on those who still revere John.[11] Again, both these sets of observations seem on the right track as far as they go, but they do not do enough to clarify the relationships and thematic structure in John 3 as a whole. Jerome Neyrey, on the other hand, has dealt with the first half of the chapter, seeing in it a confrontation between the Johannine group, with its christological testimony, and elements of the synagogue whose claims of knowledge about Jesus are rejected. Neyrey, however, follows Bultmann in attaching vs. 31–36 to vs. 1–21, thus leaving the dialogue of John the Baptist out of account in the interpretation of the chapter.[12]

It thus appears that various elements tending toward an interpretation of John 3 as a unity have been put into place, but not the unified interpretation itself. I hope in my own reading of this chapter to bring together a number of these elements, together with some new observations, in a way that can then lead toward this unified understanding of the text.

Nicodemus and John the Baptist as Communal Symbols

Let us begin with the figures of Nicodemus and John the Baptist. Each of these has been seen by a number of scholars to have significance not only as individuals but as symbols for communities or groups standing over against the Johannine Christian community. We shall first delineate these symbolic functions and then begin to explore their relation to each other and the significance of their presence together in this single chapter.

Nicodemus' role as a communal symbol has already been discussed in chapter 2 above. We may summarize our conclusions there by recalling that Nicodemus appears in the role of a "secret Christian," one of those who wish to keep their faith in Jesus, such as it is, from becoming publicly known in order to maintain what J. Louis Martyn calls a "dual allegiance" to the Christian faith and to the synagogue.[13] In particular, Nicodemus represents those secret Christians who were themselves among the Pharisaic teaching authorities and feared that a public confession of Jesus would endanger their position in the synagogue community (cf. John 3:1; 12:42). They were prepared to acknowledge Jesus, in private, as a divinely sent miracle worker and teacher, but their Christology fell short of the belief demanded by the Fourth Evangelist. For this reason, but especially for their unwillingness to let even the faith that they had be known at large, he criticized them severely. Yet even so, he evidently continued to hold some hope that they might yet come to fuller belief and to a public confession of it.

To understand this portrayal better, we must examine some of the implications of the claim in John 3:3, 7 that these secret believers need to be "born again." Jesus says to Nicodemus, "Truly, truly I tell you, unless one is born again, one cannot see the kingdom of God. . . . Don't be amazed that I told you, 'You people must be born again.'" Our first observation must be that this demand is made, not of unbelievers in the strict sense, but of people with at least some faith in Jesus. To be sure, it is implied that such half-belief is in fact little better than unbelief. But it remains true that this call is issued in what could be termed a "missionary" or "evangelistic" context only with very careful qualification.

Our second point is that, as is well known, "born again" is not an adequate translation of the phrase in question. Usage elsewhere in John shows that the meaning of *gennēthēnai anōthen* is actually "born from above," that is, from God (cf. 3:31; 19:11).[14] Hence it can be parallel to being "born of the Spirit" (3:5–8). This in turn is reminiscent of John's prologue, which calls those who received the Logos and believed in his name children of God, whose birth is not human but from God (1:12, 13). To be "born from above," then, or from God, means believing in Jesus, in the full Johannine sense, and this, as we have seen, is what Nicodemus lacks. But birth from above also means belonging to the community of such believers—we must keep in mind the plural verbs and pronouns in John 3:1–12. It is

Nicodemus' *group* that is challenged by Jesus' *group* to be "born from above" (vs. 7, 11). The reason given for this in v. 6 is that flesh gives birth to flesh, and spirit to spirit. In communal terms, this is equivalent to the declaration in 8:31–47 that physical descent from Abraham is not enough to make the hearers "children of Abraham," or of God. That is, their birth in the natural course of life ("of the flesh") has not enabled them to comprehend the one sent by God— they must be born of the Spirit, as children of God. Since it is not an individual but a group that is called upon to undergo this transformation, the implication is that these people must also break their old attachments and become adherents of the Johannine Christian group. Thus one significant aspect of the meaning of John 3:3, 7 is that the group of "secret Christians" represented by Nicodemus must both accept the christological faith of the Johannine Christians and join the group itself. To be "born from above" means not so much to have a certain experience as to take a certain action, an action with a definite communal and social dimension.[15] We will have more to say about this dimension in this chapter and in the chapters that follow.

Turning to John the Baptist, we may note that it has long been recognized that behind the portrait of him in the Fourth Gospel there lies a rivalry current in the evangelist's days between Christians and followers of the Baptist who made messianic claims on his behalf.[16] The insistence in the prologue that the Baptist himself was not the light, and the repeated avowals to the same effect placed on his own lips (1:20f.; 3:28), can certainly best be explained in this way. Even more strongly than in the Synoptics, the Baptist here hammers away at the point that after him comes one who is greater than he and that Jesus is that one (1:15, 26–27, 29–34, 36; 3:27–30). Christian Payot can even say that the Fourth Evangelist presents the Baptist as the ideal witness to Christ, a model *Christian* preacher whose one mission is to awaken faith in Jesus; and Payot rightly links this to the controversy between Christians and partisans of the Baptist.[17] Jeffrey Wilson makes this same connection with regard to John 3, where he sees the evangelist assuming the position of one who also reveres the Baptist, in order to have the Baptist repeat and affirm Jesus' testimony to himself as the one who came down from heaven. In this way John the Baptist's followers are made to hear their own master call on them to accept the claims of Jesus—or rather, the claims made about Jesus by the Johannine Christians.[18]

Thus John the Baptist also is important not simply as an individual but as evoking a group on whom the evangelist wished to press his christological claims. Unlike Nicodemus, however, the Baptist does not represent the falsehood of that group's position but rather what their true position would be if they accepted the Johannine Christians' urgings. For this reason, his disciples appear here in a body to present their unease about Jesus and to hear their master's testimony. Given the significance of John the Baptist in early Christian tradition, this is only natural.[19] John does not wish to disparage him, as he does Nicodemus, and so he must in effect set him apart from his own disciples and in opposition to them, so long as they persist in being *his* disciples and not adherents of Jesus the Lamb of God. He becomes a symbolic idealization, not of their wrongness, but of their potential rightness.

John 3 is thus concerned with two groups current in the environment of the Johannine community, the secret Christians represented by Nicodemus and the followers of John the Baptist. In the course of the chapter, both of these groups are presented with the Johannine christological claim. Nicodemus hears it from Jesus, but never accepts it. John the Baptist, on the other hand, himself lays his testimony to Christ before his disciples; but whether they accept it is not said, and they are never mentioned again in the gospel. The outlines of a thematic unity in the chapter are beginning to become clear, but in order fully to perceive it we must turn to the theme of birth from water and spirit.

Birth from Water and Spirit

When Nicodemus attempts to acknowledge Jesus as a teacher come from God, Jesus replies that in order to see the kingdom of God it is necessary to be born *anōthen*. As we have seen, this birth "from above" requires faith in Jesus, a decision in favor of him, and this is part of what sets it apart from the natural birth that is "of the flesh." Nicodemus cannot comprehend Jesus' real identity, or the nature of those who are born of the Spirit, precisely because he himself lacks this heavenly birth.[20]

But then 3:5 speaks of this as a birth from *water* and spirit, surely referring to Christian baptism.[21] Bultmann and others have sought to eliminate the reference to water as redactional, on the grounds that baptismal sacramentalism has no place in the theology of John.[22] However, the reference seems firmly anchored in the structure of John 3. For an interest in baptism is certainly not foreign to this gospel at this point: subsequently in vs. 22 and 26, and again in 4:1, we are told that Jesus himself engaged in a baptizing ministry and gained even more followers than John.[23] There can be no doubt that these statements, unique to the Fourth Gospel, are an integral part of its text. The rivalry between Jesus and John is no invention by an ecclesiastical redactor but part of a well-known Johannine theme. The Fourth Evangelist here uses Jesus' baptismal activity, most likely drawn from tradition, to build up his contrast between Jesus and John: Jesus was in fact the more successful baptizer.[24] But of course it is also stressed that Jesus, and not John, is the one who baptizes in the Holy Spirit (1:33, probably referred to again in 3:34). Thus in 3:22–4:1 Jesus is shown as the one and only one qualified to confer the birth from water and spirit demanded in 3:5. The thematic of this final demonstration of Jesus' superiority to John the Baptist would thus be incomprehensible without the reference to water baptism in 3:5.

Given the authenticity of both water and spirit in 3:5, and their significance in the overall unity of the chapter, we must go on to ask about their meaning for the two figures we have discussed. For Nicodemus, it is significant that to be born from above is not only a heavenly birth of the Spirit but also a birth of water, that is, of baptism. For baptism, it must be remembered, is not only a sacrament but an initiation rite. If to be born from above requires a decision to believe in the one sent from God, it also requires, we have suggested, adherence to the *community* of such believers. Baptismal initiation was the open declaration of this adherence, and we have seen that it was just this open confession that the group represented by Nicodemus was reluctant to make. Jesus tells them, "You people must be born from above," and that this means birth from water as well as from spirit. They cannot avoid either the christological decision or the public acknowledgment of it in baptism, that is, in initiation into the Johannine group. This social aspect of birth from water will be given further attention in chapter 4.

For John the Baptist and his followers, on the other hand, the water rite was not the new element. These disciples had had, in a sense, a birth from water in their baptism by John. But John had said that after him would come one who would baptize them in the Holy Spirit— John 1:33d surely reflects the same tradition about the Baptist's teaching as Mark 1:7–8. In the Fourth Gospel this other baptizer is revealed to John himself as Jesus, whom John then proclaims to Israel in general and to his own disciples in particular (1:29–35). It is this second baptism that John's disciples are in need of and should be awaiting, and according to the Fourth Evangelist it is available only from Jesus. He is the one who comes "from above," in contrast to the one who is "from the earth" (3:31), undoubtedly meaning the Baptist himself.[25] Therefore a birth "from above," in both water and spirit, could come only from Jesus. The followers of John are thus called upon to receive both their master's testimony, given in 3:27–36, and that of Jesus himself (cf. vs. 31–33). The closing verses of John 3 make excellent sense in their present context as a summons to the disciples of John the Baptist to accept Jesus as the Son of God into whose hands the Father has given all things, so that in this faith in him they too may have eternal life.[26] According to 3:34, "The one whom God sent speaks the words of God, for he does not give the Spirit by measure." The most natural interpretation of this is that the giver of the Spirit is God and the recipient is the one sent by God, that is, Jesus, to whom the Father has given all things (v. 35). This alludes to the descent and abiding of the Spirit on Jesus attested by the Baptist in 1:32–33, where it forms the assurance that Jesus is the one who baptizes in the Spirit.[27]

For the disciples of John, coming to faith in Jesus means coming at last to baptism in spirit and not in water alone. They, like the secret Christians represented by Nicodemus, have made the beginnings of an approach to Jesus and so to eternal life, but, like Nicodemus, they must not stop short. Their discipleship to the Baptist should lead them, not to continued devotion to him, but to faith in the one to whom he testified. Only so can they have a share in that which is "from above," a birth from both water and spirit.[28]

Conclusions

What conclusions can we now draw regarding the thematic unity of John 3? We have seen that the chapter is concerned with two specific groups, both of whom lay claim to some knowledge about Jesus, but whose knowledge is regarded as inadequate by the Fourth Evangelist. Each group has its own manner of understanding the way of God and the will of God for Israel, and neither group places Jesus at the center of its understanding, where alone he must be, according to John.

For the secret Christian Pharisees symbolized by Nicodemus, the problem is partly their fear of losing their position through a public confession of Jesus and partly their unwillingness to see in him one essentially different from themselves. They are, and wish to remain, "the teachers of Israel," and if Jesus too can somehow be fitted into this category, well and good.[29] Any radical departures—a new birth, a resurrection, a gift that transcends the law of Moses, a man who comes down from heaven—would take them beyond where they are willing to go. John 3:1–21 calls them to a spiritual and social risk that, despite their sympathy, they seem unwilling to take. They are challenged here to break with the structures of understanding into which they have sought to place Jesus, but also with the social structures in which they themselves hope to remain secure. John, or the Johannine community, is pressing upon them the claim that the action of God has taken place and is taking place not in the familiar but in the unfamiliar and the improbable. It is no wonder they hang back; but they are being warned that to hang back is to find themselves among those who avoid coming to the light because they practice wickedness and not truth (3:19–21).

How the disciples of John the Baptist actually viewed Jesus is much less clear. Perhaps they would have regarded him as a prophet, like their master; more likely, they would have seen him as a lesser figure than John. The claims being made about Jesus by Christians, and certainly those made by the Johannine Christians, would have been much more than they could allow. Yet John insists that only a positive response to those claims can fulfill their discipleship to the Baptist. What the social position of the Baptist group was in the Johannine milieu we have no way of knowing. They may not have been threatened by the authorities; or perhaps they were already separated from the synagogue community. At any rate, there is no hint that they were inclined toward belief in Jesus but reluctant to confess it because of official pressure. The Fourth Evangelist must instead urge on them the claim that the Baptist himself had pointed to another as the proper object of their hope and that he had signified Jesus as that other. They could not properly be his disciples now without acknowledging the Johannine claims about Jesus. One can imagine that the continued existence of the Baptist group was something of an embarrassment to the Johannine community. At any rate, though there is not the same sharpness in the appeal to them as in that made to the Nicodemus group, it is clear that the Fourth Evangelist saw in their reluctance to pass beyond John to Jesus an equally culpable failure to recognize the salvation of God and the one whom God had sent.

The purpose of John 3 as a whole, then, is to show the necessity of faith in Jesus in the full Johannine sense and to show that confessing this faith requires a break with rival forms of Jewish belief. Jesus can neither be tacitly fitted into the official synagogue system as the secret Christian Pharisees seek to do nor subordinated to John the Baptist as his followers do. The former group show by their limited ideas about Jesus and their refusal to acknowledge him publicly that they have not been "born from above" but have placed themselves among those who prefer darkness to light. The latter still give allegiance to the one who is from the earth, thus rejecting the testimony of him who came down from heaven and therefore rejecting God's own trueness. Both groups are in need of the new birth by both water and spirit, which is to be had only by believing in the Son of God in company with those who also believe. This intercommunal christological polemic thus provides the unifying theme for John 3, and not only links the dialogue between Jesus and Nicodemus to that between John the Baptist and his disciples but also justifies the inclusion of 3:31–36 where it now stands.

In this way we can also begin to see the compositional unity of John 3. The demand for a birth from water and spirit in 3:5 forms a kind of structural capstone uniting both halves of the text. The secret Christians stand in need of this birth in the form of a public commitment to

Jesus and the community that confesses him; the followers of John must recognize that it is not John but Jesus who is able to baptize in both water and spirit. Jesus' words to Nicodemus stand parallel to those of John the Baptist to his disciples, as Jeffrey Wilson has claimed, with the difference of course that Jesus points to himself, while John the Baptist necessarily points beyond himself. Both speeches trail off into a series of christological affirmations and warnings of the necessity of faith in Jesus because just this was precisely the point to be made to each of the two groups in question.[30] Therefore the similarities between the verses at the end of John the Baptist's speech and those at the end of Jesus' speech to Nicodemus do not indicate a displacement in the text or the work of a redactor. The text is in order as its author intended, and the similarities result from the similar aims of the two discourses, addressed to the similar needs, as the author saw them, of the two groups.[31]

Thus John has deliberately constructed and joined a matched pair of discourses on a single theme: the need to go beyond half-belief to full confession of Jesus as the Son of God come down from heaven with the gift of eternal life. The reason for this procedure was the presence in the environment of the Johannine community of two groups on the borderline between their heritage in Judaism and the Christianity of John. The Fourth Evangelist has by this means called attention to the need of both groups to break with the past, to cross the border openly and to place themselves alongside his own community. It is perhaps not accidental that the next story, in John 4, deals with another borderline group (though of a different kind), the Samaritans, and their coming to faith in Jesus. In John 2–4, John thus deals successively with a series of groups that were evidently among the most important in the social environment of the Johannine community: first the unbelieving Jews (2:14–22); then the secret Christian Jews (2:23 to 3:21); then the followers of John the Baptist (3:22–36); and finally the Samaritans (4:1–42). We have here seen one way in which our new understanding of the communal relationships lying behind the Fourth Gospel can be brought to bear on long-standing literary and exegetical problems.

NOTES

1. See Brown, *Gospel According to John,* 1:159–160.
2. Bultmann, *Gospel of John,* 131–132.
3. Schnackenburg, *Gospel According to St John,* 1:361–362.
4. Brown, *Gospel According to John,* 1:xxxvii, 160.
5. Jürgen Becker, "J 3, 1–21 als Reflex johanneischer Schuldis-

kussion," in *Das Wort und die Wörter* (ed. Horst Balz and Siegfried Schulz), 93–94.

6. Lindars, *Gospel of John,* 146–147.

7. Barrett, *Gospel According to St. John,* 219; and Haenchen, *John,* 1:209–210.

8. Dodd, *Interpretation,* 309–311.

9. Ibid., 311.

10. Meeks, "Man from Heaven," 55–57.

11. Jeffrey Wilson, "The Integrity of John 3:22–36," *JSNT* 10 (1981) 34–41.

12. Jerome H. Neyrey, "John III—A Debate over Johannine Epistemology and Christology," *NovT* 23 (1981) 115–127.

13. Martyn, "Glimpses," 112.

14. Against Bultmann (*Gospel of John,* 135). Cf. Barnabas Lindars, "John and the Synoptic Gospels: A Test Case," *NTS* 27 (1981) 290–291; Brown, *Gospel According to John,* 1:130–131; and Schnackenburg, *Gospel According to St John,* 1:367–368.

15. Cf. Meeks, "Man from Heaven," 69.

16. See, e.g., Brown, *Gospel According to John,* 1:lxvii–lxx; Schnackenburg, *Gospel According to St John,* 1:167–169; Christian Payot, "L'interprétation johannique du ministère de Jean-Baptiste (Jean I)," *Foi et vie* 68 (1969) 36; and Cullmann, *Early Christian Worship,* 60–62.

17. Payot, "Interprétation," 25–26, 29, 33–37.

18. Jeffrey Wilson, "Integrity," 39–40. Cf. Cullmann, *Early Christian Worship,* 62–63, 79–80; and idem, *Johanneische Kreis,* 64–65.

19. It is even more natural if, as several scholars have suggested, some of the early members of the Johannine community had themselves once been among the followers of John the Baptist. Cf. Brown, *Community,* 29–30; and Cullmann, *Johanneische Kreis,* 64.

20. So also Neyrey, "Debate," 120; and cf. the commentaries.

21. Other possible interpretations will be considered in chapter 4 below.

22. Bultmann, *Gospel of John,* 138 n. 3; other references may be found in chapter 4 below.

23. Strangely, John 4:2 immediately retracts the statement that Jesus himself baptized, ascribing this work to his disciples instead. Conceivably the evangelist meant in this way to avoid an identification of the mission of Jesus with that of John the Baptist (cf. Loisy, *Quatrième évangile,* 346; and Haenchen, *John,* 218). It is often suggested, however, that this awkward and contradictory explanation is the work of a later redactor (see, e.g., Dodd, *Historical Tradition,* 237, 285; Schnackenburg, *Gospel According to St John,* 1:422; and Brown, *Gospel According to John,* 1:164), and this may well be correct.

24. Cf. Dodd, *Interpretation,* 310–311; idem, *Historical Tradition,* 285–286; and Barrett, *Gospel According to St. John,* 208–209.

25. So, e.g., Brown, *Gospel According to John,* 1:160–161; Barrett, *Gospel According to St. John,* 224; Loisy, *Quatrième évangile,* 339–340; and Cullmann, *Early Christian Worship,* 80. Contrast Bultmann, *Gospel of John,* 162 n. 2; and Schnackenburg, *Gospel According to St John,* 1:383.

26. See especially Jeffrey Wilson, "Integrity," 39–40.

27. So also Cullmann, *Early Christian Worship,* 80; Schnackenburg, *Gospel According to St John,* 1:386–387; and Lindars, *Gospel of John,* 170–171. Cf. the discussion in Brown, *Gospel According to John,* 1:158, 161–162.

28. Wengst greatly misunderstands John's attitude toward the followers of the Baptist when he portrays it simply as one of sympathy for a group suffering a similar persecution (*Gemeinde,* 129–130).

29. Cf. M. Michel, "Nicodème ou le non-lieu de la vérité," *RevScRel* 55 (1981) 231, 234.

30. It therefore seems likely that 3:31–36 is intended to be understood as the continuation of the Baptist's speech and not as an address by the evangelist himself, for just here the most pointed challenge to John's disciples is given (cf. Barrett, *Gospel According to St. John,* 224; and Jeffrey Wilson, "Integrity," 37). Wilson notes ("Integrity," 39) that the expression "wrath of God" (*hē orgē tou theou*) in v. 36 is unique in the Fourth Gospel. Conceivably it is used here to give a particularly "Baptist" coloring to the concluding words of this otherwise very Johannine passage; cf. the use of the term *orgē* in the Q tradition of the Baptist's preaching in Matt. 3:7 // Luke 3:7.

It is less clear on the face of it that vs. 16–21 are to be taken as a continuation of the words of Jesus, but that would certainly contribute to the structural balance of the chapter; see the discussions in Brown, *Gospel According to John,* 1:136, 149; and Schnackenburg, *Gospel According to St John,* 1:380–381.

31. Even if the similarities result from the author's use of his own homiletical material in both cases, as Lindars suggests (*Gospel of John,* 147), the underlying reason for this parallel use would be the perceived parallelism of the situations.

4

Sacraments at the Boundary:
The Social Significance
of Baptism and Eucharist

Of the many problems that constitute the "Johannine problem," few are more complex than that of the sacraments in John. The baptism of Jesus is not narrated in this gospel, nor does Jesus command his disciples to baptize; yet in John 3, as we have seen, he declares the necessity of a rebirth from water and proceeds to baptize many people. The narrative of the Last Supper in John includes no institution of the eucharistic meal, as the Synoptics do; but John 6 claims that only those who eat the flesh of the Son of Man and drink his blood will have eternal life. What are we to make of this puzzle? Is John the most or is it the least "sacramental" of the gospels?

The issues involved are numerous.[1] To begin with, there is the problem of how Jesus is encountered in the Fourth Gospel. John is obviously concerned to elicit faith in Jesus as the Son of God incarnate. But does his concern for faith preclude a sacramental appropriation of Jesus, as Rudolf Bultmann would have it?[2] Or does his incarnational theology demand precisely that our approach to the Savior also take place through material means, as Oscar Cullmann claims?[3] Next comes the question whether the passages that seem to speak of baptism and eucharist are authentic or redactional. If they are found to be redactional, then the problem of their origin must be addressed. They might be the work of an ecclesiastical redactor alien to the Johannine tradition, as Bultmann held. Or they might come from someone within the Johannine community, either clarifying or contradicting the intention of the original gospel writer, perhaps in relation to conflicts within the community. Or they might even be the doing of the Fourth Evangelist himself, who again may have been either developing or contradicting his own earlier work.[4] On the other hand, some scholars question whether these passages are really sacramental at all, suggesting that they are to be understood symbolically, as referring to a purely "sapiential" reception of salvation through the word of Jesus; or to christological issues, Old Testament imagery, or other topics.[5] The question of sacramental symbolism in John can also be approached in still other ways—for example, by suggesting that the sacramental language is indeed sacramental but that the sacraments symbolize something else (such as the reality of Christ's incarnation); or, on the other hand, with Cullmann and others, by arguing that much that does not seem overtly sacramental is in fact part of a rich system of symbols referring to the sacraments.[6]

Once again, not all these questions will be dealt with in detail here. Rather, I intend to pose the entire problem anew from the perspective of the Fourth Gospel's communal and social environment. Some beginnings in this direction have already been made. I have mentioned conflicts within the community as a factor in some studies of the sacraments in John. These conflicts are most often seen as christological; and certainly if the sacraments are referred to at all in John, we would expect them to be strongly linked to the gospel's central christological focus. Study of Johannine conflicts has mainly centered on disputes with outsiders, especially the synagogue leaders and other Christian Jewish groups, and on the rise of docetism within the community.[7] Given the role evidently played by Christology in these conflicts, both external and internal, at least an indirect link between the sacraments and the group's social relations would not seem difficult to establish. A higher or lower Christology might lead to a higher or lower conception of the eucharist, for example, and this in turn might lead to the composition or insertion of a eucharistic passage such as John 6:51c–58 in the course of intergroup polemics.

It may also be possible to show a more direct connection, however. Research on baptism and eucharist in John has tended, naturally enough, to focus on their theological implications, whether in relation to sacramental theology or to docetic or antidocetic Christology. Not surprisingly, and not necessarily wrongly, scholars' own theological commitments and overall understandings of Johannine theology have often tended to sway the exegesis of particular passages. This, given the difficulties inherent in the text, readily makes for the kind of impasse described above. But baptism and eucharist have other ramifications besides the purely "sacramental" or "theological." For studies such as that of the Pauline communities by Wayne Meeks have shown that early Christian baptism and eucharist also functioned socially to establish and maintain both group boundaries against the outside world and internal group cohesion.[8] Since boundaries and cohesion are prominent aspects of the social issues that have been

identified by research on the Johannine community, it may be possible
to make progress in verifying baptismal and eucharistic references in
John and in understanding their significance in the Johannine setting
on this basis. In the past the focus on "sacramentalism" or its absence
in authentically Johannine theology has obscured the existence of
other possible areas of meaning for baptismal and eucharistic language. My contention will be that such language may be present and
may refer directly and primarily to the rites in question without their
nature as "sacraments" being its chief subject.[9] If instead their social
function is what is chiefly in view, then it may be that their presence
would not offend against "Johannine theology" at all, whether or not
that theology is regarded as essentially sacramental in nature. Indeed,
as we shall see, baptism and eucharist treated in this way may be
positively related to some central features of John's theology.

Let me note at the outset several limitations to this study. Though I
use the term "sacraments," my subject is more precisely "baptism and
eucharist." I regard as untenable the notion that other "sacraments"
can be found hinted at in John.[10] Moreover, it should be evident that
by "sacraments" I refer primarily to the rites as such, not to their
theological significance or interpretation. But it should also be evident
by now that I do not consider social and theological analysis to be
mutually exclusive. On the contrary, my theme is precisely that our
theological understanding of John may now be subject to revision
through our new awareness of the social background of this gospel.
Finally, I should remark that my study will be limited to the *loci
classici* concerning baptism and eucharist in John: the dialogue with
Nicodemus, in particular John 3:5; and the discourse on the Bread of
Life, particularly 6:51c–58. In these passages, we will consider both
the authenticity of the sacramental references and their meaning in the
light of the Johannine communal situation.

Baptism

A great variety of interpretations have been offered for the expression "born of water" in John 3:5.[11] As we have seen, Bultmann and a
few others reject it as a piece of later ecclesiastical redaction, out of
keeping with the nonsacramental nature of Johannine theology.[12]
Other scholars have sought to demonstrate that "water" here does not
refer to baptism at all.[13] We need to examine both of these positions
before attempting to speak of the social implications of being "born of
water."

The notion that "water" does not refer to baptism has never
commanded wide scholarly support, though it has appeared from time
to time in various forms. Some of these treat "water" and "spirit" in

John 3:5 as referring to two separate births, of which that by water is the old and that by spirit the new. The most common suggestion has been that "water" refers to natural birth, either to male semen[14] or, more frequently, to the amniotic fluid that is discharged during childbirth.[15] One scholar, however, has proposed that "water" symbolizes the Jewish religion, whose adherents, represented by Nicodemus, need a further birth from the Spirit.[16] Aside from the weakness of the linguistic evidence cited in support of these interpretations, two chief objections may be noted. In the first place, they overlook the baptismal context in John 3:22–26; 4:1–2, as discussed in our preceding chapter. Second, they ignore the fact that birth from water is, just as much as birth from spirit, part of the condition for entering the kingdom of God in John 3:5. There is surely no sense in saying that one must be born, physically, to enter the kingdom of God, since every conceivable hearer already has been; and no more sense in telling a "teacher of Israel" that he must be a Jew.[17] On the whole, it seems impossible for any interpretation to make sense of the passage by separating birth from water and birth from spirit.

Slightly more promising are other studies that see in "water" a reference to Old Testament imagery for the Spirit itself, perhaps in relation to hopes for an eschatological act of cleansing.[18] "Water and spirit" thus becomes a kind of hendiadys, referring to the spiritual regeneration now available in Jesus. But these proposals too neglect the baptismal context. Like the others, they seem largely to proceed from a recognition that the historical Jesus can hardly have spoken to the historical Nicodemus about Christian baptism, and from a corresponding desire to save the historicity of the dialogue itself.[19] We may acknowledge the unlikelihood of the historical Jesus' making such a statement about baptism. What we must investigate is the sense it would make as a statement of the *Johannine* Jesus.

Before that, however, we must be sure that the statement is authentically Johannine. Objections to it have been met in one respect by Cullmann, Helmut Köster, and Raymond Brown, who all stress that, even without the mention of water, baptism could be suggested by the dialogue's theme of rebirth, since a connection between the two is frequently made elsewhere in early Christian literature.[20] In any case, in chapter 3 above I have shown the originality of the baptismal motif, based on its significance for the contrast between Jesus and John the Baptist in John 3. What was said there about the significance of a birth from water for the group that Nicodemus represents may be taken as further confirming the authenticity of the reference to baptism in 3:5. We may now proceed to develop those observations further, in a way that should both strengthen our confidence in the baptismal reference and deepen our understanding of its sense.

The difficulty that has led some scholars to deny the authenticity of the word "water" in John 3:5, and others to deny that it means baptism, is the apparent incongruity of the baptismal reference. Ignace de la Potterie holds that "water," which is not found again in the context, breaks the continuity of the original literary structure.[21] For Bultmann, a reference to baptism would separate the verse from what follows it and confuse the thought of vs. 6 and 8, since John "rejects the sacramentalism of ecclesiastical piety."[22] Eduard Lohse does not claim that John opposes the sacraments but that he concentrates everything on the word of Jesus. Reference to a sacrament here would degrade the new birth from a miracle of God's sovereign revelation, creating new life where it will, to something attainable through ritual and hence under merely human control.[23] Those who hold that "water" refers to something other than baptism likewise assert the irrelevance of baptism at this point.[24]

This apparent irrelevance is an illusion. It results in part, as already noted, from neglect of the baptismal references in the context outside the dialogue with Nicodemus. But it also arises from considering baptism only as a sacramental ritual. What we must do is take account of the social significance of baptism in the Johannine milieu.

Though there is indeed no further mention of a sacramental rite in the dialogue, the problem of a boundary between two groups is of its essence. It is a dialogue between a "we" and a "you people," concerning who "knows" and whose testimony is to be accepted. The author repeatedly uses exclusive formulations: "unless one . . . one cannot" (*ean mē* followed by a negative apodosis [vs. 3, 5]), or "you people *must* be born from above" (v. 7). As John 1:12–13 reminds us, this birth that comes from God was available only to those who "received" the incarnate Logos, who "believed in his name." Thus the christological issue between the Johannine community and the secret Christians looms powerfully behind the discussion of birth "from the spirit."

The interest in baptism is therefore of a very particular sort, closely linked to the intergroup rivalries in which the Johannine community was embroiled. As we saw in chapter 3 above, it is not only the christological confession but the water that separates the Johannine community from the crypto-Christians. Barnabas Lindars regards baptism here as the decisive response to the word about Jesus, equivalent to a confession of faith in the full Johannine Christology.[25] Evidently those who fell short of this confession also declined to take the step of baptism into full membership in the community. We may compare John 12:42, where open confession occupies a place analogous to baptism in 3:5 as a dividing line between the Johannine community and crypto-Christians in positions of power who were afraid to acknowledge their faith. Baptism is thus viewed in John in the same light as public confession, as an acknowledgment of adherence both to Jesus as divine Son of God and to the community whose testimony to him is thereby accepted. It forms a boundary between those inside the believing community and those outside it, and to be baptized is to cross that boundary in an openly recognizable way. To be "born from above" is to undergo a change of communal affiliation and is therefore a social as well as a spiritual event.

Clearly this conception of baptism corresponds well to a number of aspects of baptismal function described for the Pauline communities by Wayne Meeks. There too baptism forms a threshold between the world and the community where Jesus is Lord, and there too baptism is associated with the reception of the Spirit and becoming a child of God. In both cases, baptism accomplishes the transition from the world to an exclusive community and thus serves as a permanent boundary between the two.[26]

To cross this boundary between outside and inside by baptism has, for John as for Paul, more than purely theoretical consequences. For "they will put you out of the synagogues; indeed, the hour is coming when everyone who kills you will suppose he is offering a service to God" (John 16:2). Baptism represented a change of social location for the Johannine Christians, and not necessarily one for the better. Closely linked to christological confession, to hearing and accepting the word of Jesus, baptism also possessed this unavoidable social dimension. To be "born from water and spirit" meant not only a sacramental regeneration—indeed, that may be one of the less prominent aspects of baptism in John 3—but everything that birth can mean, a new foundation, a new beginning, both spiritual and social, in a totally new world.

The new birth thus has its expression in this choosing and declaring of sides at the boundary. Spiritual birth is indeed given by God, and, as Lohse remarks, it is experienced "where God's revelation is accepted in believing obedience."[27] But this obedience is a *public* obedience, and Johannine faith includes an element of public attestation. This is seen in the portrayal of Nicodemus throughout the Fourth Gospel. In need of the birth of water and spirit, he was evidently not among the many baptized by Jesus (or by his disciples), according to John 3:22, 26; 4:1–2. One time, timidly and without effect, we see Nicodemus defending Jesus before his fellow Pharisees—but not taking the extreme step of confessing his own faith and his own adherence to the "mob that does not know the law" (7:45–52). He is not heard when the blind man is interrogated and expelled, when the decision is made to put Jesus to death, when Jesus himself is on trial. Not until Jesus is sadly—but safely—dead does Nicodemus again appear, with his great burden of burial spices to dignify the great teacher's corpse. Nicodemus endeavors not to choose, or not to declare his choice, until it is too late to matter. That is why he is confronted with the birth from *water* and spirit: the water of baptism symbolizes and embodies the act of choice and declaration. Since it is this act which stands between the Johannine community and the secret Christians, the water, and the rite of baptism to which it refers, is immovably rooted in the dialogue with Nicodemus, not as a sacramental ritual but as the social boundary that confronts Nicodemus and that he is challenged to cross.

We must not, and do not, forget that "born from water and spirit" is an expansion of "born from above" and is itself summarized as "born from the Spirit." What is involved is not merely a human act of decision or an initiatory rite. John, at any rate, claims it is a gift of God. But we must remember that it is not the new birth itself but the newly born *people* who in John 3:8 are said to be a mystery to the world, as incomprehensible to it as the wind.[28] Nicodemus is obviously no mystery to the world; indeed, those born of the Spirit are a mystery to him. It is this origin in God's Spirit that makes them opaque to the world, which does not know and cannot receive the Spirit (14:17). This evidently sectarian attitude toward the world we will explore further in later chapters. What we must note here is that although those who are born of the Spirit may be incomprehensible to the world in their origin and their destiny, nevertheless it "hears their sound." Birth from above is not an invisible event, unknown to anyone but the individual in question. It alters that person's place in the world and stance toward the world, or it has not taken place at all, and it aligns him or her with others who have become equally unfamiliar to the world. If it were only a birth from spirit, it might not be so, but it is so because it is a birth from *water* and spirit.

Eucharist

In turning to John 6, one must first admit that the authenticity of the eucharistic passage in 6:51c–58 is far more in doubt than that of "water" in John 3:5. Questions about the genuineness of these verses have arisen from such factors as the shift of focus from faith in Jesus (as in the earlier parts of the Bread of Life discourse) to eating his flesh as the means of obtaining eternal life; the crassly material way in which this eating is apparently conceived; the change from Jesus as the bread given to Jesus as the giver of bread; and indeed the eucharistic emphasis as such in contrast to the remarkable absence of the institution of the eucharist from the Last Supper narrative in John.[29]

Some scholars also object to various stylistic elements in the passage as non-Johannine, but these arguments are more difficult to evaluate.[30]

The issues involved are too many and too complex to weigh every argument presented by every scholar on the subject. Though I do not believe that full certainty can quite be attained, I do think it possible to argue that the passage belongs here as a part of the original work of the Fourth Evangelist, on the basis of its content, its structural relation to its immediate surroundings, and its relation to other Passion materials that are seemingly "displaced" in the Fourth Gospel. I hope to show this, as compactly as possible, in the section that follows. It may be convenient first, though, to give a translation of the entire passage.

> [51]"I am the living bread that came down from heaven. If anyone eats of this bread, that person will live forever; and the bread that I shall give is my flesh for the life of the world." [52]So the Jews disputed with one another, saying, "How is it possible for this man to give us his flesh to eat?" [53]So Jesus said to them, "Truly, truly I tell you, unless you eat the flesh of the Son of Man and drink his blood, you do not have life in you. [54]Whoever eats my flesh and drinks my blood has eternal life, and I will raise that person up on the last day. [55]For my flesh is true food, and my blood is true drink. [56]Whoever eats my flesh and drinks my blood abides in me and I in that person. [57]Just as the living Father sent me and I live because of the Father, so also whoever eats me will live because of me. [58]This is the bread that came down from heaven, not as the fathers ate and died. Whoever eats this bread will live forever."

The authenticity of John 6:51c–58

The content of the passage is evidently eucharistic, but it has sometimes been brought into relationship with the problem of docetism, that is, the idea that the divine Christ only appeared to take on mortal flesh, but was not truly human. This in turn has various possible implications for the authenticity and meaning of the passage. Thus several scholars, while accepting its authenticity, have suggested that its primary purpose has to do not with the eucharist as such but with antidocetist polemic. Peder Borgen claims that the eucharistic motifs are used merely to illuminate the reality of the incarnation.[31] J. D. G. Dunn argues that the author's primary goal is to oppose a docetic Christology but that he also opposes a too highly sacramental *anti*docetism, his use of eucharistic language being purely secondary and metaphorical.[32] Yet even Dunn must admit the presence of this eucharistic language, and it seems impossible that any Christian writer or reader could have construed the vivid demand in 6:53–56 to "eat the flesh of the Son of Man and drink his blood" as anything other than the strongest sort of invitation to the eucharistic meal.

The possibility of antidocetic intention in the passage has also been raised by some who accept both its authenticity and its eucharistic focus. Cullmann, for instance, sees the stress on the materiality of the sacrament as corresponding to a Johannine emphasis on the reality of the incarnation and the flesh of the Logos.[33] Wilhelm Wilkens recognized the fully sacramental character of the passage but saw the sacramentalism as of a thoroughly Johannine sort, regarding it as part of the Fourth Evangelist's own transformation of his work into an antidocetic Passion gospel.[34] Yet even in this form the antidocetist theory seems untenable to me, simply because the traces of antidocetism in the Fourth Gospel are too weak to sustain it, particularly in comparison with the Johannine epistles. Neither John 1:14 nor 19:34–35 contains a consciously antidocetist polemic, though of course both could be *used* against docetism. In general, the Fourth Gospel is too concerned with proving the divinity of Jesus to pause for a demonstration of his real humanity. If there was a controversy over docetism in the Johannine community, it seems to have arisen after the work of the gospel writer was finished, and it is the epistles that bear the strongest witness to it.[35]

Perhaps then we should give greater credence to those who see antidocetism in John 6:51c–58 and for that very reason regard the passage as inauthentic and interpolated. Georg Richter and Hartwig Thyen, for instance, like Wilkens, suggest that docetic Christology would have been linked to a docetic concept of the eucharist that devalued its real material consumption. For them, however, this docetism grew up within the Johannine community after the completion of the gospel and led to its editing and interpolation in an antidocetic direction. Richter, like Günther Bornkamm and others, compares the resulting antidocetic sacramentalism of 6:51c–58 with that of Ignatius of Antioch.[36]

The difficulty with all these views is their claim that the opponents being addressed in the passage were supporters of an overly exalted docetic Christology and indeed (for some scholars) that they came from within the Johannine community itself. The actual addressees in the text, however, are not the disciples (who do not appear with their objections until v. 60) but "the Jews." And if there is anything about John that is absolutely certain, it is that "the Jews" do not stand for proponents of a high Christology, let alone for inner-Johannine docetists, but for "the world" that rejects precisely the exalted Johannine christological claim. Nor is it only docetists who might oppose a strong view of the eucharist. Those who did not share the high Johannine Christology might equally well have regarded the eucharist as no more than a memorial meal in honor of a great teacher. Hence the disciples who turn away in 6:60, if they are to be seen as associated with "the Jews," must be regarded as holding unacceptably *low* views of both Christology and the eucharist, as Raymond Brown has suggested.[37]

Those who hold the antidocetic view of 6:51c–58 propose, as Thyen in particular stresses, that the focus of these verses is Christology more than eucharistic doctrine as such.[38] But what is the christological issue here? The claim in these verses seems to be that the eucharist is Jesus' flesh and blood and therefore can give eternal life—not because it is flesh and blood but because it is *Jesus'* flesh and blood. I would agree with Ulrich Wilckens that the issue is not the docetic one of the material reality of the eucharist but rather the claim that the eucharist as the *Son of Man's* flesh and blood is true, reliable food and drink (6:55).[39] Jesus' exalted status as life-giver is essential to this conception and is thus integral to the polemic in the text. There is indeed a christological issue associated with the eucharistic theme, but that issue is not necessarily docetism. The eucharist as such is not viewed as a "medicine of immortality," in Ignatian terms, but is related to the high Johannine christological claim, and thus is kept well within the bounds of known Johannine concerns. I would argue, then, that 6:51c–58 opposes a low, not a high, Christology, and for precisely that reason may be regarded as authentically Johannine.

The question of the passage's relation to its immediate surroundings is, if anything, even more complex. Bultmann is followed by many in defining the eucharistic section as beginning at v. 51c, "And the bread that I shall give is my flesh for the life of the world."[40] Yet at least an equal number of scholars, of the most diverse schools of thought regarding other issues in the passage, locate its beginning at or around v. 48, with its clearly resumptive repetition from v. 35 of "I am the bread of life."[41] It may well be that a new paragraph does begin with this verse, but it is not at all clear that the discussion of the eucharist begins already here. Heinz Schürmann's demonstration that v. 51c itself, though based on eucharistic tradition, refers in this context primarily to Jesus' death as the giving of his flesh for the life of the world is a strong one.[42] Thus vs. 48–51 may be taken as a return to the subject of the true bread of life in contrast to the manna,[43] with the added turn now given that Jesus is this bread precisely in the giving up of his life on the cross. The eucharistic section proper begins only with the question of "the Jews" in v. 52 and the reply in vs. 53–58.[44]

In support of this it must be noted that if the subject of the eucharist begins already with the words "The bread that I shall give is my flesh," then "the Jews'" question, "How can this man give us his flesh to eat?" has rightly understood those words as referring to the eucharistic meal. But the sense of the passage seems much more to be that this question is a misunderstanding, which nevertheless says more than the questioners realize. The fact is that up to this point Jesus has *not* said that he will give them his flesh to eat, only that they must eat of the Bread of Life and that the bread he will give is his flesh (v. 51). As elsewhere in John, Jesus' opponents leap to a conclusion that is wrong, and yet perversely and profoundly right (cf. 7:35; 8:22, 53), and Jesus proceeds to repeat his offending statement in a more offensive form yet. Their uncomprehending question is seized on to show that "the Jews" have spoken more truly than they know, in that *Jesus'* flesh and blood, taken in the eucharist, is a really worthwhile food and drink. In the structure of this misunderstanding there are significant parallels to the dialogue with Nicodemus.[45] We will discuss these later in the chapter. Their presence, along with the general structure of misunderstanding followed by more radical claim, serves to strengthen the likelihood that this passage derives from the Fourth Evangelist himself.

With regard to the verses following 6:58, Bornkamm endeavored to show that the offense to Jesus' disciples and the mention of "flesh" in 6:60–63 refers, not to the eucharistic passage, but back to the Bread of Life discourse itself.[46] Other scholars, however, have preferred to follow the more obvious line of interpretation which sees in the scandalizing and departure of some of the disciples in 6:60–71 a result of the "hard" eucharistic words, and an interpretation of these words in the pronouncement that "the flesh is of no benefit."[47] The point is a significant one, for, as Bornkamm observes, these verses make difficulties for the interpolation hypothesis, since they would require that a still later interpolator have inserted them as commentary on the previous addition. Even if Bornkamm were correct, however, it would only imply that the eucharistic redactor had chosen an inconceivably inept place for his interpolation.

How may we understand John 6:60–71, then, in relation to the eucharistic passage? An important clue is given by Kikuo Matsunaga, who points out the connection of the scandalized disciples to the traitor Judas and concludes that both stand for Christians who had broken with the Johannine community because they held a lower (not a higher)[48] Christology than John.[49] This is consonant with what was argued above concerning the tendency of 6:51c–58 itself, and aligns the disciples who do not believe (v. 64, in contrast to v. 69) with "the Jews" of the eucharistic passage. It would imply that John is here defending his high Christology, in itself and in its implications for the eucharist, not only against the synagogue but also against Jewish Christian opponents. With Matsunaga, the "word" of Jesus that gives life (vs. 63, 68) is the Johannine christological kerygma. As "spirit" it is contrasted with the "flesh" to show that what gives life is not the eucharistic elements themselves, however they are conceived, but the faith that sees in them the Son of Man, the exalted Johannine Jesus.

Thus 6:51c–58 does fit into its context in John 6. The discourse proceeds from a general presentation of Jesus as the Bread of Life come down from heaven through a typically Johannine misunderstanding to an even more offensive explication of John's Christology in relation to the eucharist. It ends in a critique of Jewish Christians who were unable to accept either the Christology or its eucharistic implications. The christological theme is thoroughly Johannine and does not suggest an interpolation.

But why is this discussion of the eucharist placed here rather than at the Last Supper? This is actually a greater problem for those who attack the authenticity of the passage than for its defenders. For if an ecclesiastical redactor or an antidocetist within the Johannine community had wanted to add a eucharistic passage, why would the addition not have been made at the obvious point, the Supper narrative in John 13? If one could explain the location of the eucharistic discourse as a part of the author's original plan, it would be quite significant, since no adequate reason has ever been given for a *redactor's* placing of it at such an inappropriate point.[50]

What is too seldom observed in this regard is that the eucharistic material is not the only matter "displaced" in John which belongs, in the Synoptic tradition, to the time in Jerusalem immediately preceding the Passion. The cleansing of the Temple, for instance, is pushed all the way up to John 2. The decision to put Jesus to death is linked to the raising of Lazarus (11:47–53), the anointing at Bethany takes place before the triumphal entry (12:1–8), and even the agony in the garden is clearly echoed in 12:27–28, prior to the Last Supper. Indeed, the interrogation concerning Jesus' messiahship and the charge of blasphemy found in the Synoptic account of Jesus' trial may be reflected already in John 10:24, 33. Of course these transpositions, especially that of the cleansing of the Temple, are commonly noted and explained in relation to John's theology and literary history in the commentaries.[51] But only one scholar has seen the value of accounting for all of them by a single hypothesis. Wilhelm Wilkens, along with Schürmann and others, regards 6:51c as having its origin in a version of the institution of the eucharist such as is found in the Synoptic Last Supper narrative.[52] But Wilkens saw the displacements of the Temple cleansing, the eucharistic words, and the anointing all as the result of the Fourth Evangelist's reworking of his original gospel, which was much more like the Synoptics in outline, in order to bring the entire narrative under the sign of the Passion of Jesus. (As noted above, Wilkens saw John's motive for this in a growing antidocetism.)[53] Much of Wilkens' work is far too ingenious to be convincing, and perhaps for that reason it has been neglected. Certainly the antidocetic motivation is much too weak to explain why the evangelist should literally turn his gospel inside out. Nevertheless, there is great value in his attempt to explain the "displacements" of numerous elements of the pre-Passion narrative together as the result of a single theological and literary move. The making of a "Passion gospel" seems to me motive enough in itself to account for the present arrangement. In Wilkens' words, "In the present gospel, the Passion narrative begins, not with chap. 13, but already in chap. 2. . . . The entire messianic work of Jesus in deed and word is now incorporated into the Passion narrative."[54]

But this act is more likely to have been envisioned by the author from the beginning of his work than by a redactor (even the author himself) after its completion. If John was conceived from the first as a Passion gospel, the evangelist may have taken elements familiar to him (and his community) from the Passion tradition and scattered them about in this way to achieve a particular goal. Namely, the confrontation with the world that ended Jesus' life is now made to characterize his entire life. The idea of his rejection by "his own" to whom he came in revelation (1:11) is dramatized in the Passion, and the dramatization distributed throughout the entire gospel. John is a Passion gospel precisely because of this intimate connection in Johannine thought between the revelation of Jesus to the world and his Passion. It is his revelation that leads to the Passion, and the Passion is the climax of his revelation. This is abundantly clear in some of the displaced Passion scenes, notably the Temple cleansing and the "trial" scene in 10:22–39. But it is also relevant to the eucharistic passage, following as it does on the themes of revelation and rejection in the Bread of Life discourse. Jesus gives life to the world by giving his own flesh on the cross. In rejecting this act, the world only brings its rejection of his entire revelation to a head. The eucharist, representing the gift of life in his flesh, is thus also an apt object of the world's rejection, and so it is portrayed here.

At any rate, this hypothesis allows us to avoid multiplying ad hoc explanations for the placement of each of these items and to see the whole as part of a single intention. It accounts for the presence of the eucharistic passage in John 6 and its absence from John 13 without recourse to a nonsacramental (or antisacramental) gospel and an obscurely motivated redactor. It may also help us later on to interpret certain other evident connections between this passage and the Johannine Last Supper narrative.

We may summarize this lengthy (but still far from exhaustive) excursus on the authenticity of John 6:51c–58 by saying that the passage makes sense here both as a part of John 6 and as a part of the

Fourth Evangelist's overall plan. Its content is coherent with John's christological concern to proclaim the identity of Jesus as the divine Son of Man come down from heaven with the gift of eternal life, and in particular with his defense of this confession against those who rejected it. That is the overall theme of the Bread of Life discourse, and the eucharistic passage does not deflect from it. Rather, it carries this theme forward into the realm of the Christian eucharistic meal. It does so as part of a larger intention to present the work of Christ under the aspect of the cross. As Schürmann and others have shown, one major emphasis of the Bread of Life discourse, including the eucharistic passage, is the death of Christ as the indispensable source of the world's life.[55] The eucharist is transposed here from its place in the Passion tradition because of its obvious relevance to the miracle of the loaves (which itself has, even in John, eucharistic overtones).[56] Thus, here as elsewhere, the Fourth Evangelist means to say that it is precisely the shamefully crucified Jesus who is the life-giving Son of God. Even his crucifixion, *precisely* his crucifixion, does not refute but confirms the truth of Johannine Christology. What we must now examine is the relation of this claim, as expressed in the eucharistic discourse, to the social setting of the Johannine community.

The social significance of the Johannine eucharist

In discussing the authenticity of John 6:51c–58, we have already noted some ways in which groups in the Johannine milieu may be relevant to the understanding of the passage and its context. In particular we concluded that, if the passage has reference to intergroup christological disputes, it is more likely to have been directed against a low than a high or docetic Christology.

We also remarked in passing that there are a number of noteworthy parallels between the dialogue in John 6 and the dialogue with Nicodemus. In both, an initially not unfriendly interlocutor proves unable to comprehend Jesus' words and is increasingly distanced from him. In both, the climactic question is "How is it possible?" (*pōs dynatai*, John 3:4; 6:52). And in both, this question is met with an "Amen, amen" saying cast in the form of an exclusive formulation: "Unless one is born from water and spirit, one cannot enter the kingdom of God" (3:5); "Unless you eat the flesh of the Son of Man and drink his blood, you do not have life in you" (6:53). We have earlier seen that in John 3 the formulation is used in a context where the boundary between two groups forms part of the subject matter and where a factor in this boundary is christological, the refusal of the outsiders to accept the Johannine claim about Jesus. The same usage is evident again when a similar formula is used in John 8:24b: "Unless you believe that I am he, you will die in your sins."[57] Thus we would expect that in the eucharistic passage too, division, between those who accept the Johannine christological claim and those who do not, between those who eat the flesh of the Son of Man and drink his blood and those who do not, is under discussion. Participation in the eucharist is here made a criterion for inclusion in or exclusion from "life" in a manner that brings its function as a boundary into prominence. Since the eucharist is exclusive to the Christian community, full and open adherence to that community is implicit in the eucharist's role in defining those who have life.

We have also discussed the eucharistic pericope's relationship to other "displaced" Passion texts in John and remarked that the passage probably derives from an "institution narrative" at the Last Supper. Now we must turn to some often-noted parallels between it and the Farewell Discourses of John's Last Supper narrative.[58] John 6:56, "Whoever eats my flesh and drinks my blood abides in me and I in that person," calls to mind 14:20, "I am in my Father and you in me and I in you," and even more strongly 15:4–7, with its repeated variations on "Abide in me and I in you." The next verse (6:57), "Just as the living Father sent me and I live because of the Father, so also whoever eats me will live because of me," is also paralleled in the same contexts. In John 14:19b we read, "I live and you also will live", and in 15:9–10, "As the Father has loved me, I also have loved you. . . . If you keep my commandments, you will abide in my love, as I have kept my Father's commandments and abide in his love" (note also 17:18, 23; 20:21). This suggests that the author, in moving the eucharistic material to this location, meant it still to be interpreted in connection with the Farewell Discourses, whose matter may have been well known in the Johannine community even though not all of it was incorporated in the first edition of the gospel.[59] Then either the author meant that the Farewell Discourses should be reinterpreted along the lines of a crassly materialist sacramentalism, which seems most unlikely, or else he meant that the Farewell Discourse material should influence the interpretation of the eucharistic passage.

If the latter is the case, we may follow its implications a bit farther. In John 14:18–24, the mutual indwelling and shared life of Jesus and his disciples is associated with Jesus' revelation of himself to those who love him and keep his commandments when the world sees him no more. Likewise in 15:4–17, the reciprocal abiding includes Jesus' words abiding in the disciples and leads to a discussion of keeping his commandments, namely, the commandment of love. Fernando Segovia has argued that this love commandment is a secondary addition, related to the later docetist schism in the Johannine community.[60] However, it seems more likely that 15:1–17 is to be read as a complement to the following section, 15:18–16:4a, which warns of hatred and persecution by the "world," that is, by the synagogue authorities. My reasoning is as follows. Segovia may be right that "love" for Jesus and "keeping his word" means holding the Johannine christological faith in Jesus (cf. 8:42, 51; 16:27), and the same for "keeping his commandments" in John 14.[61] Note also that John 15 begins with a stress on *abiding in* Jesus, which undoubtedly means abiding in the christological confession, that is, the same thing that is elsewhere called "keeping his commandments." Only then does it expand the idea of abiding in Jesus' love and keeping his commandments into that of loving one another. Whence does the need for this mutual love arise, and how is it related to the confession of Jesus? The clue is found in 15:18–16:4a, where the disciples (i.e., those who believe in Jesus, keep his commandments) are the object of the world's murderous hatred. From this would come the possibility, under persecution, of giving one's life for one's friends as Jesus did—that is, of loving one another as Jesus loved his disciples (15:12–13). I would suggest that even if 15:1–17 and 15:18–16:4a are of independent origin, they arrived in this location simultaneously, as deliberate complements. Both are authentic Johannine material, from the same stage of communal history—namely, the conflict with the synagogue.[62] The injunction to love one another reflects the conditions of the Johannine community drawn together into communal solidarity in the face of the hostility of the unbelieving world.[63] Their love for one another indicates the reality of their faith in Jesus, just as the world's hatred of them reflects its rejection of him.

This is the context within which we must read the eucharistic passage, given its parallels to John 14 and 15. According to 6:56, those who eat and drink the eucharist abide in Jesus and he in them. This must be understood in relation to the Johannine communal setting, in which the solidarity of individuals with Jesus, their "abiding" in him, was of hard necessity closely bound up with their solidarity with one another, their "love." To abide in Jesus, that is, to maintain the Johannine christological confession (with which, as we have seen, the eucharistic passage is closely connected), meant to be distanced and isolated from the social world of the synagogue. The risk that this involved we have already found portrayed in the figures of Nicodemus, the blind man, and the blind man's parents. John 16:2 suggests that the risk could have extended in some circumstances to life itself. In these conditions, the need for mutual support would have been strongly felt, and it seems clear that the members of the Johannine community were in fact tightly drawn together. "Love" would mean not only affection and a general kindliness but standing with others in the community against betrayal by outsiders and participating actively in creating the new communal bonds that must take the place of the lost synagogue fellowship. The eucharist symbolizes not only the gift of eternal life in Jesus but also the world's rejection of that gift and of the community that had accepted it. If sharing in the eucharistic meal meant affirming the Johannine faith, it would also have meant affirming the community's solidarity in the face of the dangers brought upon them by their faith.

Similarly, according to 6:57 the life the individual receives from Jesus is the life that Jesus received from the living Father, and we must recall that in the Farewell Discourses it is this same paradigm that determines and undergirds relationships among individuals in the community. The Father loved Jesus, and in the same way Jesus loved the disciples. He kept the Father's commandments and so abode in his love: likewise the disciples are to keep Jesus' commandments and so abide in his love. And the commandment in particular that they are to keep is that they love one another as Jesus loved them (15:9–13). Receiving the Father's life from Jesus, associated with the eucharist in John 6:57, brings to mind this paradigm and therefore the mutual love that is to characterize relationships within the community. Moreover, the life that they receive from Jesus is part of what distinguishes them from the world, which does not "see" him as they do (14:19).[64] It should be stressed again that it is not the sacrament itself but the person of Jesus that is decisive in this giving of life. His flesh and his blood are true, reliable food and drink because they are *his:* "Whoever eats me will live because of *me"* (6:55, 57b). It is not the rite as such that brings life but the communion with Jesus that it affords.[65] Therefore to partake in the rite is implicitly to accept the Johannine community's claim that Jesus is the source of life, the life that he received from the Father to give to the world. Thus the eucharist, like baptism, symbolizes open adherence to that claim, which is itself the great boundary line that separates the Johannine community from the world. The eucharist in its own way thus serves to recall and reinforce that boundary. Both the individualism and the "sacramentalism" of the eucharistic passage are mitigated by these parallels to the Farewell Discourses.

We have seen that the focus of the eucharistic passage John 6:51c–58 is as much christological as it is sacramental and that this christological focus places the eucharist in the context of that which separates the Johannine community from the world and unites its members with one another. This christological center and certain parallels with the Nicodemus dialogue suggest that the eucharist, like baptism, is part of what effects the division of the Johannine community from the world and particularly from the synagogue community. Moreover, by enacting the believers' union with Jesus, the eucharist reinforces not only their location within the community and separation from the world but also the mutual solidarity within the group. This solidarity, the love that those who abide in Jesus have for one another, is the necessary concomitant of their alienation from those outside. The Johannine eucharist thus serves to strengthen both the internal solidarity of the group and its boundaries against the hostile world. As with baptism, these functions correspond to those served by the eucharist in the Pauline churches, as Wayne Meeks describes them, although they are manifested in very different ways in the texts.[66]

Conclusions

It is clear by now that the "sacraments" of baptism and eucharist need not be viewed as alien to the thinking of the Fourth Evangelist. On the contrary, they are closely linked to the christological and communal issues that were paramount among his concerns.

The eucharist in particular testifies to the believer's acceptance of Jesus as divine life-giver, and both baptism and eucharist represent public acts of adherence to the community within which Jesus is confessed as Son of God come down from heaven. Like the confession itself, these acts separate the community and its individual members from the outside world, and this is the aspect of them that seems to interest the gospel's author, as much as if not more than their sacramental character in the strict sense. Baptism represents the threshold between the world and the community for John, and also the risk of crossing that threshold. The eucharist reinforces this boundary, too, and is linked to the maintenance of solidarity within the community of those who faithfully abide in Jesus and remain faithful in love to one another. If John says that one must be born of water as well as spirit to enter the kingdom of God, and must eat the flesh and drink the blood of the Son of Man to have eternal life, in neither case is this an act performed by the individual in isolation from others. If these are transactions between the individual and God, they are also public and social transactions. They serve to bring the individual among a group of others, and to inaugurate and maintain two precisely defined relationships, one of separation from the world and the other of love and union with these others.

NOTES

1. Cf. the surveys of research in Raymond E. Brown, "The Johannine Sacramentary," in *New Testament Essays,* by Raymond E. Brown, 51–56; and Herbert Klos, *Die Sakramente im Johannes-*

evangelium, 11–44. Regrettably, the work of Klos is in general too derivative to be of great value here.

2. Bultmann, *Gospel of John,* 219; and idem, *Theology of the New Testament,* 2:58–59. Cf. also, e.g., Eduard Lohse, "Wort und Sakrament im Johannesevangelium," *NTS* 7 (1960–1961) 110–125.

3. Cullmann, *Early Christian Worship,* e.g., pp. 76, 95–97, 99–100, 118.

4. Ecclesiastical redactor: Bultmann, *Gospel of John,* 138 n. 3; Helmut Köster, "Geschichte und Kultus im Johannesevangelium und bei Ignatius von Antiochien," *ZTK* 54 (1957) 62; and Robert Kysar, *The Fourth Evangelist and His Gospel: An Examination of Contemporary Scholarship,* 251, 254.

Redactor within the Johannine community: Lohse, "Wort und Sakrament," 120; Günther Bornkamm, "Die eucharistische Rede im Johannes-Evangelium," *ZNW* 47 (1956) 162–164, 169; idem, "Vorjohanneische Tradition oder nachjohanneische Bearbeitung in der eucharistischen Rede Johannes 6?" in *Geschichte und Glaube,* 2:52–54, 61–64; Sydney Temple, "A Key to the Composition of the Fourth Gospel," *JBL* 80 (1961) 222–232; Hartwig Thyen, "Entwicklungen innerhalb der johanneischen Theologie und Kirche im Spiegel von Joh. 21 und der Lieblingsjüngertexte des Evangeliums," in *L'Evangile de Jean: Sources, rédaction, théologie,* (ed. Marinus de Jonge), 259–299; idem, "Aus der Literatur zum Johannesevangelium (4. Fortsetzung)," *ThR* 43 (1978) 337–341, 349; idem, "Aus der Literatur zum Johannesevangelium (5. Fortsetzung)," *ThR* 44 (1979) 97–99, 108–109; and Georg Richter, "Zur Formgeschichte und literarischen Einheit von Joh 6, 31–58," in *Studien zum Johannesevangelium,* by Georg Richter, 88–119.

Fourth Evangelist the redactor: Raymond E. Brown, "The Eucharist and Baptism in John," in *New Testament Essays,* by Raymond E. Brown, 86–92; idem, *Gospel According to John,* 1:287–291; Wilhelm Wilkens, "Das Abendmahlszeugnis im vierten Evangelium," *EvTh* 18 (1958) 354–370; and idem, *Die Entstehungsgeschichte des vierten Evangeliums,* 20–24, 75–77, 125. Cf. Ignace de la Potterie, " 'To Be Born Again of Water and the Spirit'—The Baptismal Text of John 3,5," in *The Christian Lives by the Spirit,* by Ignace de la Potterie and Stanislaus Lyonnet, 1–36 (originally in *Sciences ecclésiastiques* 14 [1962] 417–443), who holds that John revised his own pre-gospel tradition.

5. See the references in nn. 13, 31, and 32 below.

6. R. Wade Paschal, Jr. ("Sacramental Symbolism and Physical Imagery in the Gospel of John," *Tyndale Bulletin* 32 [1981] 151–176) decides in favor of the former position. For the latter position, see Cullmann, *Early Christian Worship,* 37–119, and others discussed in

Brown, "Sacramentary," 54–56, 66–75; and Klos, "Sakramente," 24–37.

7. See the studies referred to in chapter 1 above, especially those of Brown, Martyn, Meeks, de Jonge, Smith, Thyen, Richter, Segovia, Woll, and Whitacre.

8. Wayne A. Meeks, *The First Urban Christians: The Social World of the Apostle Paul,* 153–160.

9. Indeed, Barnabas Lindars has with good reason cautioned against any application of the category "sacraments," in its developed sense in Christian theology, to John or to the New Testament writings in general ("Word and Sacrament in the Fourth Gospel," *SJT* 29 [1976] 49–52).

10. See the discussions cited in n. 6 above.

11. Cf. the surveys in Linda Belleville, "Born of Water and Spirit," *Trinity Journal,* N.S. 1 (1980) 125–134; and de la Potterie, "Born Again," 1–12.

12. Bultmann, *Gospel of John,* 138 n. 3; Lohse, "Wort und Sakrament," 116; F.-M. Braun, "Le Don de Dieu et l'Initiation Chrétienne," *NRT* 86 (1964) 1033–1037.

13. E.g., D. G. Spriggs, "Meaning of 'Water' in John 3⁵," *ExpTim* 85 (1973–1974) 149–150; Margaret Pamment, "John 3:5," *NovT* 25 (1983) 189–190; Ben Witherington, "The Waters of Birth: John 3.5 and 1 John 5.6–8," paper read at the Society of Biblical Literature annual meeting, Atlanta, Ga., Nov. 23, 1986; D. W. B. Robinson, "Born of Water and Spirit," *Reformed Theological Review* (Australia) 25 (1966) 15–23; Zane C. Hodges, "Water and Spirit—John 3:5," *BSac* 135 (1978) 206–220; and Belleville, "Born of Water and Spirit," 128–130, 134–141.

14. A possibility raised, and rejected, by Barrett, *Gospel According to St. John,* 209.

15. See the articles by Spriggs, Pamment, and Witherington (who allows for either possibility) cited in n. 13 above.

16. D. W. B. Robinson, "Born of Water and Spirit."

17. Cf. Hodges, "Water and Spirit," 211–213.

18. See the articles by Hodges and Belleville cited in n. 13 above.

19. Cf. Belleville, "Born of Water and Spirit," 129.

20. Cullmann, *Early Christian Worship,* 75–78; Köster, "Geschichte," 63–64; and Brown, "Eucharist and Baptism," 93–94. This of course might only confirm the motivations of the supposed ecclesiastical redactor.

21. De la Potterie, "Born Again," 23.

22. Bultmann, *Gospel of John,* 138 n. 3.

23. Lohse, "Wort und Sakrament," 116, 125.

24. Spriggs, "Meaning of 'Water,' " 149; D. W. B. Robinson, "Born

of Water and Spirit," 15; and Belleville, "Born of Water and Spirit," 129.

25. Lindars, "Word and Sacrament," 55–56.

26. Meeks, *First Urban Christians,* 151–157.

27. "Wo Gottes Offenbarung im glaubenden Gehorsam angenommen wird" (Lohse, "Wort und Sakrament," 116).

28. Or as Jesus himself: cf. 3:8 with 7:27–29; 8:14; 9:29; 19:9.

29. Cf. Bultmann, *Gospel of John,* 218–220; Haenchen, *John,* 1:296–300; Lohse, "Wort und Sakrament," 117–120; Bornkamm, "Eucharistische Rede," 162–163; and Richter, "Formgeschichte," 39–44.

30. Lohse ("Wort und Sakrament," 118–119), e.g., argues that the style is not Johannine; Eduard Schweizer ("Das johanneische Zeugnis vom Herrenmahl," *EvTh* 12 [1953] 353–354) argues that it is. Many scholars have been persuaded by the arguments of Eugen Ruckstuhl (*Die literarische Einheit des Johannesevangeliums,* 243–271) that the style of the passage is in fact Johannine. Günther Bornkamm, on the other hand, declares that such criteria are not probative, since *anyone* using Johannine thought and language, as the author of 6:51c–58 does, will end up sounding "Johannine" ("Vorjohanneische Tradition," 53).

31. Peder Borgen, *Bread from Heaven,* 186, 189–190.

32. J. D. G. Dunn, "John vi—A Eucharistic Discourse?" *NTS* 17 (1970–1971) 328–338, esp. pp. 332–337.

33. Cullmann, *Early Christian Worship,* 99–100.

34. Wilkens, "Abendmahlszeugnis"; and idem, *Entstehungsgeschichte,* 20–24.

35. Cf. Brown, *Gospel According to John,* 1:1xxv–1xxvii; and idem, *Community,* 93–144, esp. pp. 109–120.

36. Richter, "Formgeschichte," 43–48; Thyen, "Entwicklungen," 277; "Aus der Literatur" (*ThR* 43) 341; "Aus der Literatur" (*ThR* 44) 98, 108–109, 121; Bornkamm, "Eucharistische Rede," 163, 169; and idem, "Vorjohanneische Tradition," 61–64. On the relation to Ignatius, see also Köster, "Geschichte."

37. Cf. Brown, *Community,* 74–75, 78 n. 145.

38. Thyen, "Aus der Literatur" (*ThR* 44) 109; cf. Dunn, "John vi," 335–336.

39. Ulrich Wilckens, "Der eucharistische Abschnitt der johanneischen Rede vom Lebensbrot (Joh 6,51c–58)," in *Neues Testament und Kirche* (ed. Joachim Gnilka), 237–239.

40. Bultmann, *Gospel of John,* 218–219, 240.

41. As only a few examples, see Cullmann, *Early Christian Worship,* 95; Bornkamm, "Vorjohanneische Tradition," 59–61; Thyen, "Aus

der Literatur" (*ThR* 43) 340; idem, "Entwicklungen," 277; Borgen, *Bread from Heaven*, 87–88; and Wilckens, "Eucharistische Abschnitt," 222–226. For some other references, see Brown, *Gospel According to John*, 1:293–294.

42. Heinz Schürmann, "Joh 6,51c—ein Schlüssel zur grossen johanneischen Brotrede," *BZ*, N.S. 2 (1958) 244–262.

43. Cf. Richter's demonstration, against Borgen, that vs. 48–51b round off the preceding discourse rather than beginning a new section ("Formgeschichte," 23–31).

44. Cf. Barrett, *Gospel According to St. John*, 296.

45. Cf. Schweizer, "Johanneische Zeugnis," 359.

46. Bornkamm, "Eucharistische Rede," 164–168.

47. Bornkamm is followed by Richter, "Formgeschichte," 51–52; Thyen, "Entwicklungen," 277; Wilckens, "Eucharistische Abschnitt," 243–245; and Brown, *Gospel According to John*, 1:299–300 (contrast Brown, *Community*, 74!). The contrary is held by Schweizer, "Johanneische Zeugnis," 357–358; Wilkens, "Abendmahlszeugnis," 363–364; Dunn, "John vi," 330–332; and Barrett, *Gospel According to St. John*, 302 (who points out that "flesh" in v. 63 is all the more likely to refer back to the repeated use of that term in vs. 51c–58, since it does not occur previously in the chapter).

48. As claimed by Thyen, who discusses this passage in "Entwicklungen," 277–280.

49. Kikuo Matsunaga, "Is John's Gospel Anti-Sacramental?" *NTS* 27 (1981) 516–524. Cf. also Brown, *Community*, 74, 78–79, where this group is treated as composed of Jewish Christians totally outside the Johannine community.

50. Richter's attempt to account for it on the basis of the docetists' supposed use of the Bread of Life discourse ("Formgeschichte," 46–47) is entirely speculative.

51. E.g., Brown, *Gospel According to John*, 1:117–118, 287–290 (cf. idem, "Eucharist and Baptism," 86–88); Schnackenburg, *Gospel According to St John*, 1:344–355; Barrett, *Gospel According to St. John*, 195; Lindars, *Gospel of John*, 136–137, 379–382, 545–546; idem, *Behind the Fourth Gospel*, 62, 70, 75; and Cullmann, *Early Christian Worship*, 74.

52. Wilkens, "Abendmahlszeugnis," 355; idem, *Entstehungsgeschichte*, 75–77; and Schürmann, "Schlüssel," 246–248; cf. Brown, *Gospel According to John*, 1:287; and idem, "Eucharist and Baptism," 86–88.

53. Wilkens, *Entstehungsgeschichte*, passim, esp. pp. 9–24, 91, 123–126; and idem, "Abendmahlszeugnis," 367–369.

54. "Im Jetztevangelium beginnt die Passionsgeschichte eben nicht

erst mit Kap. 13, sondern schon in Kap. 2! ... Das ganze Christuswerk Jesu in Tat und Wort wird nun in die Passionsgeschichte einbezogen" (Wilkens, *Entstehungsgeschichte,* 68, 123).

55. Schürmann, "Schlüssel," passim; and Schweizer, "Johanneische Zeugnis," 359–361.

56. Cf. Brown, "Eucharist and Baptism," 82–84; and idem, *Gospel According to John,* 1:247–248.

57. We may also note similar usages in 13:8 and 15:4, 6, whose examination, however, would take us too far afield here.

58. See, e.g., Brown, *Gospel According to John,* 1:283; Loisy, *Quatrième évangile,* 462; and Lindars, *Gospel of John,* 269. For Richter, these parallels serve to confirm the secondary nature of the eucharistic passage ("Formgeschichte," 37, 40).

59. Cf. Brown, *Gospel According to John,* 1:xxxvi–xxxvii; 2:586–587; Lindars, *Gospel of John,* 467–468, 486; Barrett, *Gospel According to St. John,* 545–546; and Schnackenburg, *Gospel According to St John,* 3:90–95.

60. Fernando Segovia, *Love Relationships in the Johannine Tradition,* 101–121.

61. Segovia, *Love Relationships,* 146–153; and idem, "The Love and Hatred of Jesus and Johannine Sectarianism," *CBQ* 43 (1981) 258–272.

62. A suggestion I owe to Frank S. Thielman, "Inside or Outside? An Assessment of Recent Research on the Purpose of the Fourth Gospel," paper read at the Society of Biblical Literature Southeast Regional meeting, Chattanooga, Tenn., March 21, 1986.

63. The connection between persecution and communal solidarity, i.e., love of one another, is also drawn by Wengst (*Gemeinde,* 123–124) in relation to John 13:34–35.

64. On the syntax of this verse, see Barrett, *Gospel According to St. John,* 464; and cf. Brown, *Gospel According to John,* 2:640.

65. Cf. Wilckens, "Eucharistische Abschnitt," 237–239; Paschal, "Sacramental Symbolism," 166; and Cullmann, *Early Christian Worship,* 95–99. On the translation of 6:55, see Schweizer, "Johanneische Zeugnis," 360; and Schnackenburg, *Gospel According to St John,* 2:62–63.

66. Meeks, *First Urban Christians,* 159–160.

5

The Trial of Jesus
and the Politics of John

In his study of the feeding of the multitude in John 6, C. H. Dodd showed that the crowd's attempt to make Jesus king (6:14–15) fits the turbulent political conditions of pre-70 Palestine better than any subsequent period.[1] We also find the interesting statement in John 11:48 that the chief priests and the Pharisees were afraid that Jesus' large following might bring down the wrath of the Romans on Jerusalem. Taken together, these passages present a clearer and probably more realistic picture of how Jesus would have appeared in the pre-70 political situation in Palestine than anything that is found in the Synoptic gospels. Dodd attributed the political awareness of 6:14–15 to the independent tradition behind the gospel rather than to the evangelist himself, suggesting that one of the characteristic features of the distinctive Johannine tradition was an attention to Jewish messianic politics not typical of other sectors of early Christianity.[2] In this, Dodd may well have been correct. If so, however, it is conceivable that such an interest may have continued to characterize the Johannine community and the Fourth Evangelist himself. At any rate, there is no reason to dismiss the suggestion out of hand. For John, of course, this would represent not just a concern for historical detail but a further feature of his christological portrait of Jesus and the world that rejected him. Nevertheless, the possibility is raised that Christology and politics were not completely unrelated for the Fourth Evangelist.

Consistently with this, the political nature of the charges against Jesus is given far more emphasis in the Fourth Gospel than elsewhere in the New Testament. The term *basileus*, "king," for instance, occurs twice as often in John's account of the trial of Jesus as in the corresponding section of any of the Synoptics. The centrality of political issues in the Johannine trial narrative has in fact often been noted.[3] Usually, however, John's interest in these issues is seen as apologetic, like that of the other evangelists and the early church generally: he wished to relieve the Romans of responsibility for the death of Jesus and to assure them that despite appearances to the contrary, neither Jesus nor the church was a political threat to the Empire.[4] Exceptions to this view have been very rare.[5] Yet certain features of John's presentation invite the question whether his attitude toward Rome was necessarily as conciliatory as Luke's, for instance, is often said to have been. Certainly the early church was not absolutely monolithic in this regard, as the book of Revelation shows, and we are now well aware of the idiosyncrasy of the Johannine community within early Christianity.

It is thus reasonable to inquire about the position of the Fourth Evangelist in relation to the political situation facing Jews and Jewish Christians in the period after 70 C.E. First, though, we must remind ourselves briefly of what that situation was. We are mainly concerned with attitudes toward the Roman government and not with Jewish internal politics. However, the emergence of the Pharisees during this period as the primary group from prerevolutionary times with the ambition and the means to lay claim to leadership within the Jewish community was not without larger political dimensions. Morton Smith has long since shown that Josephus' account of the Pharisees in the *Antiquities* was designed to commend them to the Romans as the one party commanding the popular allegiance to maintain stability in Palestine.[6] Similarly, Jacob Neusner has brought out the part played by R. Yohanan ben Zakkai and men like him in creating a postwar structure for Judaism, dedicated to the cultivation of Torah piety, that could both meet with acceptance from the Romans and ensure the survival of the Jewish people. The Pharisees thus presented themselves as *the* agents through whom Rome could and must deal in order to achieve the pacification of the Jews, accommodating themselves to Roman rule as they gained the ascendancy in the guidance of Judaism, which they now steered toward a concentration on religious faithfulness.[7]

But it should not be thought that hopes for deliverance from Roman rule were merely sublimated by these means. Yohanan ben Zakkai himself died with hope for the Messiah on his lips (*'Abot de Rabbi Nathan* 25a). The Eighteen Benedictions with which he and his colleagues at Jamnia concerned themselves contained prayers for the restoration of Jerusalem, the Temple, and the house of David, and rabbinic tradition carefully preserved the rules for the conduct of the Temple against its expected reconstruction. Apocalyptic works continued to express vivid anticipations of the messianic overthrow of Roman power (see 2 Esdras 11–13; *2 Baruch* 39–42; 63; 82).[8] Indeed, such works show that the very movement toward piety and penitent obedience to God was oriented toward the hope of political deliverance: "The messianic hope was a remarkable mixture of political and religious ideals. . . . The political freedom of the nation which they longed for was viewed as the goal of God's ways."[9] And of course it was the redoubtable sage Akiba himself who declared, in the face of opposition, that Simeon ben Kosiba—Bar Kokhba—was the King Messiah (*y. Ta'anit* 68d). Nor were such hopes absent in the Diaspora. Josephus' *Jewish War* had been written with the aim of convincing Jews abroad that Galilee and Judea had been wrong to rebel; but the *Sibylline Oracles* mourned the destruction of the Temple and looked for the coming of the Messiah and God's judgment on the Gentiles and restoration of Jerusalem (4.2.5–4.3.1 §§115–126, 4.3.10 §§171–192, 5.9.4–5.10.3 §§403–433). Within a decade or two at most after the writing of the Fourth Gospel, violent messianic rebellion broke out among the Jews of Cyrenaica and Egypt and then spread to Cyprus and Mesopotamia (115–117 C.E.).[10] It is possible that this revolt aroused sympathetic uprisings in Palestine and that preparations for the rebellion under Bar Kokhba began there only a short time later.[11]

Such, then, is the political background against which the gospel of John must be viewed. There was accommodation to Roman rule in some quarters, an attempt to provide a peaceful framework within which Jewish faithfulness could be maintained and elaborated in the new situation. There were others, however, in whom the political and religious aims that had inspired the Maccabees and the Zealots remained alive. We know little about their activities in detail; yet during these years the seeds of the Bar Kokhba revolt lay germinating in the ashes of Jerusalem.

This chapter will examine what the political implications of the Johannine trial narrative would have been in such a context, focusing especially on the scenes before Pilate. I will not be looking for historical remains of the actual trial of Jesus but will be analyzing the intention of John himself by studying the way he has treated his material. I do not presuppose any detailed source theory for the Johannine Passion narrative. I do presume, as usual, that John did not use any of the Synoptics but rather a tradition or traditions essentially independent of them.[12] This tradition, as suggested above, may already have taken a notable interest in the political aspects of Jesus' trial. Whatever his sources may have been, however, John has thoroughly reworked them, so that no exact reconstruction of them seems necessary here. I will note in general terms what items are likely to have been traditional, but our main attention will be given precisely to those things for which the Fourth Evangelist himself seems responsible, especially the arrangement of the material and the speeches of the various characters.

My contention will be that John's handling of the story must be studied in relation to the concrete political climate of the late first century in order to appreciate his true intentions. Pilate, for example, is hardly likely to represent an abstract philosophical construct, "the state," for John;[13] but he may well represent the *Roman* state, a real and already hostile power that evoked both submission and passionate resistance in John's Jewish and Christian contemporaries. Observing Pilate's role in the Fourth Gospel in this light may thus help us to grasp what it was that John meant to convey by portraying him as he does. In this way I hope to open up one more of the levels of meaning in John's narrative. I do not claim that John's interests here are exclusively political. The uppermost issues are certainly theological, and these of course have always been given close attention.[14] Yet the title "King of the Jews," accorded such prominence in John, necessarily has political connotations, whatever its significance for Johannine Christology. I intend to show that in the late first century C.E., when Jewish and Christian theology and politics could seldom be totally separated, the author of the Fourth Gospel had a distinctive conception of what those connotations were.[15]

Jesus' Arrest and Preliminary Interrogation: John 18:1–24

The distinctive features of John's account can already be seen in the story of Jesus' arrest. Only in this gospel do the Roman cohort and its commander appear alongside Judas and the Jewish officers in the garden (18:3, 12).[16] Whether the whole six-hundred-man cohort or only a detachment is understood to be involved is of little moment for us,[17] as is the question whether they are the evangelist's invention or were already present in the tradition he received.[18] The fact is that there is an official Roman interest in the arrest of Jesus from the very beginning in the gospel of John. If this interest was already there in the tradition John used, then at the very least he has made no effort to obscure it, as the Synoptics are sometimes said to have done; and it remains possible that he has actually introduced the Romans of his own accord.

The scene with the high priest which follows, in which Jesus defiantly refuses to discuss his teaching (18:19–23), is probably meant to be paradigmatic for the Christians of the Johannine community, in a manner similar to the story of the blind man in John 9.[19] Like Jesus and like the blind man (and in sharp contrast to the denial of Peter), they are to give uncompromising testimony when called before the

Jewish authorities. But perhaps the most noteworthy feature at this point is that, in contrast to the Synoptic narrative, no Jewish court ever formally charges or condemns Jesus, nor do Jews administer any beating or mockery (beyond the single slap in 18:22). "The Jews," of course, have been virulently hostile to Jesus throughout the gospel, and many commentators see the lack of a Sanhedrin trial here as indicating that Jesus' debate with them has already been concluded.[20] Yet though their instigation of his trial and execution is left in no possible doubt, the omission of the Sanhedrin trial rests the *formal* responsibility for the humiliation and condemnation of Jesus squarely on the Roman prefect Pilate.

Up to this point, then, the gospel of John allows for far more official Roman involvement in the proceedings against Jesus than do the Synoptics. There is no exculpation of the Romans at the expense of the Jews. The Fourth Evangelist shows Jesus heatedly refusing to cooperate in his interrogation by Jewish authorities, and yet this does not result in any official verdict against him on their part. If it is correct to suppose that the general inclination of early Christianity, including the Synoptic gospels, is toward an apologetic aimed at improving relations with the Roman government, then John at least does not share in that inclination, and we shall be justified in reading the rest of his trial narrative without necessarily expecting to find it there.

The Trial Before Pilate: John 18:28–19:16

The careful crafting of Jesus' trial before Pilate in the Fourth Gospel has often been observed. The narrative is divided into seven well-balanced scenes, alternating between interviews with "the Jews" outside the praetorium and interior episodes involving Jesus and Pilate or the soldiers.[21] Some of the elements found here and there (whether historical or not) were certainly present in the tradition before John, such as the charge of blasphemy leveled against Jesus, the reluctance of Pilate to condemn him, and the politically charged question, "Are you the King of the Jews?" Often enough John seems to presume that his readers already know the basic story. Yet the arrangement as a whole is artificial and tendentious, and the exact nature of John's "tendency" must be sought precisely in his very artful construction of the story. Moreover, John is the supreme ironist among New Testament writers, and it is always dangerous to attempt to read his meaning naively off the surface.[22] Careful attention must be given to the dramatic values of the narrative and to the motives of the three main characters, Pilate, "the Jews," and Jesus. Of these, it is Pilate who links the whole together. We will begin by following his actions through the story, and after that turn to the others.[23]

Pilate

By virtually universal consent, Pilate is seen in John as a more or less sympathetic figure, a man who wants to be fair, who would gladly acquit Jesus, but who through lack of resolve and susceptibility to political pressure all too easily becomes the tool of "the Jews" and their malevolence. Along with this goes the usual view of John's purpose as apologetic: Pilate is portrayed as Rome's representative convinced of Jesus' political innocence and sincerely trying to let him go.[24] At the very worst he is seen as representing the divinely legitimated state, which, through a misplaced effort at neutrality, forgoes its chance to stand for God and so inevitably loses control of events to the world, the forces of darkness.[25] Yet even those who accept this understanding have noted some problems with it. Pilate's repeated ironic references to Jesus as "King of the Jews" seem calculated more to embitter "the Jews" against Jesus than to win his release.[26] His motive for scourging Jesus in the middle of the proceedings remains very obscure.[27] Pilate is supposedly the weak figure, harried by the implacable "Jews"; but surely their final exclamation in 19:15 ("We have no king but Caesar!") is precisely in accord with Roman desires, so that in the end it is Pilate, not "the Jews," who emerges triumphant.

It may be worth the effort, then, to try reading the Johannine Pilate as a strong character rather than a weak one. The Christian portrayal of Pilate as it had developed by the late first century (exemplified by Matthew and Luke) contained an obvious contradiction in the reluctance of the prefect to crucify Jesus, which nevertheless must result in his crucifixion. It may be that John has seen and capitalized on this contradiction, so that for him it is turned to irony, and Pilate too becomes an agent of "the world," instead of a good-hearted but inexplicably impotent governor. Certainly it would be possible in John for a character to proclaim Jesus' innocence without himself believing in it or caring about it. Such, I hope to show, is Pilate. He is undeniably hostile to "the Jews," but that does not make him friendly to Jesus, for whose innocence he is not really concerned. Rather, his aim is to humiliate "the Jews" and to ridicule their national hopes by means of Jesus.[28] A careful reading of the text will support this interpretation.

Pilate at first declines any involvement with the case but agrees to take jurisdiction when "the Jews" inform him that it is a capital matter (18:31). If there is an apologetic note in Pilate's diffidence and "the Jews'" insistence, [29] it is balanced by the fact that in spite of their refusal to name any specific charges (18:29–30) he is at once willing to proceed with the hearing when he learns that a crucifixion is in the offing.[30]

In Pilate's first interview with Jesus, which follows in 18:33–38a, the framework (consisting of Pilate's question, "Are you the King of the Jews?" and Jesus' reply, *su legeis,* "You say it") is traditional,[31] but the substance is thoroughly Johannine. Pilate's relationships with the other characters begin to become plain here. His contemptuous "Am I a Jew?" (v. 35) identifies him at once as their antagonist, at least on the surface.[32] His questioning of Jesus remains narrowly focused on the subject of kingship, while Jesus, in typically Johannine fashion, raises the issues past Pilate's comprehension. Nor is Pilate's final "What is truth?" the question of a serious seeker; if it were, he would stay for an answer.[33] According to 18:37, those who are of the truth, rather than of this world, listen to Jesus: the Roman is not interested. Thereby, as Wayne Meeks points out, Pilate answers his own question from v. 35: he would deny it (*mēti*), but he is ranked alongside "the Jews" among those who do not hear Jesus' voice.[34] He is "of the world."[35]

Pilate's declaration that Jesus is innocent and the Barabbas scene with his offer to release Jesus (18:38b–40) again come from tradition. John, however, trims them down considerably[36] and in so doing makes the declaration of Jesus' innocence largely subordinate to the offer to release him (vs. 38–39). Yet it is difficult to give full credence to Pilate's offer, since he already knows what "the Jews" want to do with Jesus (18:31). Why should he ask them now if they want him released? Therefore it is also not quite possible to trust his intentions when he declares that he finds Jesus innocent. Nor is his slightly sardonic reference to "the King of the Jews" likely to win "the Jews" over to Jesus' side.[37] We gain the impression that Pilate is merely going through a formality, well aware of what the outcome will be.

In any case, the sequel totally undermines his pronouncement that Jesus is innocent and shows that this innocence is a matter of indifference to him. For when "the Jews" refuse to accept his proposed release of Jesus, Pilate at once sends him to be scourged (19:1), a procedure that should not properly be used on a guilty man until he has been formally condemned,[38] let alone on one who has just been declared innocent. The scourging and the mockery are thus, in spite of all historical probability, made the central of John's seven scenes. John does this deliberately to set the stage for his final dialogues in which the relationships among Pilate, "the Jews," and Jesus are brought to a climax. For it is the mock-king, scourged and crowned with thorns, that Pilate now brings before "the Jews."

The scourging of Jesus might seem to suggest that Pilate is ready to gratify "the Jews'" desires,[39] but this is not so. His intention is not to placate them but to humiliate them.[40] None of his posturing about "the King of the Jews" or Jesus' innocence from this point on can be taken seriously. His statements are all ironic taunts, and he uses Jesus to make a ridiculous example of Jewish nationalism. Thus in 19:4 he *says* that he is bringing Jesus out to show that he has found him innocent, but the absurdity of this is deliberately underlined in the following verse when the scourged Jesus comes out "wearing the crown of thorns and the purple robe." At one level, Pilate may indeed mean that he finds no guilt—and no threat—in this ludicrous figure, in whom he portrays just how preposterous he finds the idea of a Jewish "king." At a deeper level, of course, John's irony stands the mockery of Pilate on its head: this is in truth the king, and this is his royal epiphany.[41] "The Jews," of course, do not see this. They see only the bitter burlesque of Jewish royalty, and neither Pilate nor the reader could seriously expect them to respond otherwise than as they do.[42] "Behold the man!" he says, and *now,* beholding him, the chief priests cry out, "Crucify!" (19:5–6). Pilate's next suggestion, that "the Jews" crucify Jesus themselves, is again contemptuous. He knows perfectly well that they have no such authority. They have told him so in 18:31, and he himself asserts his jurisdiction in 19:10. He is merely driving home to them their lack of national sovereignty: take him and crucify him yourselves, if you are a sovereign nation and have laws—and a king—of your own.[43] Of course this "offer" is tantamount to releasing Jesus,[44] which is neither here nor there to Pilate but causes "the Jews" to insist that they do have a law and that Jesus really does deserve to die (19:7). Here for the first time they bring before Pilate the charge of blasphemy that they have held against Jesus all along: "He claimed to be Son of God."

Only John among the New Testament gospels has this claim mentioned to Pilate. His own christological presentation demands that it be so; but the pagan Pilate is brought up short by it: *mallon ephobēthē,* "he became fearful instead" (19:8).[45] *Mallon* here cannot mean that Pilate became "more" afraid—he has not been afraid up until now.[46] The word can mean "instead," or even just "exceedingly."[47] His fear serves to move the scene back indoors for one last testimony to the supremacy of Jesus (19:9–11, to be discussed below). This appears to have its effect, for now, for the first and only time, Pilate seriously tries to release Jesus. Again, the wording is noteworthy: *ek toutou,* "at this"—but *only* at this—*ezētei apolysai auton,* "he *began* seeking to release him" (19:12).[48]

"The Jews," perhaps sensing that they have taken the wrong tack, now revert to the political issue (19:12–16), and in the strongest terms: "If you release this man, you are no friend of Caesar." The question of Jesus' divinity, which had served to motivate Pilate's reluctance to condemn him, vanishes at once, and with it Pilate's reluctance. At "the Jews'" words Pilate resumes his former character, produces both Jesus and the judgment seat (whoever it may be that sits on it),[49] and again confronts them with their ravaged "king," this time insisting on giving him title and all. They respond as before, but Pilate repeats the taunt, with an irony that can hardly be missed: "Am I to crucify your king?" This final thrust elicits from them at last an abnegation of their highest national hopes: "We have no king but Caesar"; and Pilate, having heard the one thing that he has been waiting to hear, hands over Jesus with alacrity.

This last outcry by "the Jews" is the climax of the trial scenes. It is what Pilate has been driving them toward, and if it seals their fate in the mind of the Fourth Evangelist, it does so only by aligning them with Pilate himself, for whom also there can be "no king but Caesar."[50] The Roman prefect is thus by no means a man of just intentions but weak character in this gospel. He is callous and relentless, indifferent to Jesus and to truth, and contemptuous of the hope of Israel that Jesus both fulfills and transcends. He grants "the Jews" their desire but exacts an intolerable price from them. This is fully confirmed in the incident of the title on the cross (19:19–22), when Pilate refuses to modify his grimly ironic captioning of the crucified Jesus as "King of the Jews." In this, as in his "Behold your King" (19:14), Pilate of course is one of those unconscious witnesses in the Fourth Gospel who say more than they know; but this makes him no better than Caiaphas (cf. 11:49–52).[51] Pilate is thus in fact a hostile figure second only to "the Jews" themselves. His sin may be less than theirs (19:11), but it is sin nonetheless. Moreover, by having him bully "the Jews" into accepting the kingship of Caesar, the evangelist shows himself implicitly critical of that kingship. Certainly he does not agree with Pilate and "the Jews" that Israel has no king but Caesar, and this must make him inimical not only to Pilate but inevitably also to the system that Pilate represents. This conclusion will be further justified as we look at the story from the viewpoints of the other characters in it.

"The Jews"

It is a commonplace of interpretation that "the Jews" in John represent the world that rejects the revelation of God in Jesus. We have also seen that they stand for the Jewish opponents of the Johannine community, and in the trial scenes the evangelist uses the political aspect of the charge against Jesus as a bludgeon against these opponents. "We have no king but Caesar," uttered, as John is at such pains to point out, just as the observance of Passover begins,[52] is a renunciation of Israel's profession to have no king but *God,* as made in the Passover hymn *Nishmat kol hay,*[53] but also as made by the Zealots precisely in their struggle against Caesar.[54] John would hardly have been unconscious of this. With this cry, "the Jews" reject the kingship not only of Jesus but of God as well. In its stead they accept only the kingship of this world, and with it Caesar's claim to divinity, so that for John it is they who are the true blasphemers. The failure on the part of "the Jews" is thus a spiritual one;[55] but it is a political failure too, and John seems to feel the bitterness of it on both counts.[56] Moreover, their rejection of their king takes place precisely when they see him humiliated by Pilate: if *this* is the King of the Jews, then "the Jews" will have none of him. If they are to have a king, it must not be one who can be dealt with in this way. Indeed, they have already preferred Barabbas the *lēstēs* (the "robber," i.e., revolutionary) over Jesus, suggesting that their coerced submission to Caesar is not entirely wholehearted.[57]

John may thus have been making his own way among ambivalent political tendencies in the Jewish community between the two revolts. For him, once the true King of Israel had appeared, both the continued expectation of a revolutionary Messiah and the accommodation of the emerging Pharisaic leadership to the reign of Caesar were abhorrent. The rejection of Jesus by "the Jews" reaches its climax in the shout "We have no king but Caesar!" and this fact suggests that although the coming of the Son of God in John transcends all expected messianic categories, the bearing of the messiahship of Jesus on Israel's political life is by no means obliterated.

Jesus

Jesus' interviews with Pilate very likely represent a model for the Johannine community's dealings with Roman officials,[58] just as Jesus' interrogation by the high priest reflects the community's relationships with the Jewish authorities (as noted above). The attitude depicted is certainly not one of abject submissiveness, though an apologetic function for some of his words can perhaps be surmised. Thus in the first dialogue (18:33–38), when Pilate asks Jesus whether he is the King of the Jews, Jesus turns the question aside by asking whether Pilate is speaking of his own accord or at the prompting of others. The Roman is thus reminded that the "kingship" of Jesus was of no interest to him until "the Jews" raised the question; so why should he be concerned about it now? Later, Pilate is reminded that Jesus' followers do not fight to prevent his betrayal to "the Jews" (18:36)— they present no threat of armed revolt.[59]

But this verse will bear closer examination. Jesus says that the lack of violent resistance on his servants' part proves that his kingship (not kingdom) is not of this world. However, what is not of the world may nevertheless be in the world, as Jesus and his followers are (see 17:14–18), and Jesus' words about his kingship do not deny that it *is* a kingship, with definite social characteristics. Instead, they specify what those characteristics are. It is not a question of *whether* Jesus' kingship exists in this world but of *how* it exists; not a certification that the interests of Jesus' kingdom are "otherworldly" and so do not impinge on this world's affairs, but a declaration that his kingship has its source outside this world and so is established by methods other than those of this world.[60] Indeed, as Heinrich Schlier observes, Jesus' kingship, though rooted in the coming world, nevertheless exerts its peculiar authority already over this one.

> The testimony that Jesus . . . gives thus does not deny that he, Jesus, has a sovereign domain in this world. It also says, however, that this realm does not have its roots in this world. Thereby, however, it sets before the world a sovereignty that fundamentally surpasses every other. . . . Jesus' kingdom shows that it is not bound to the world in that he, its king, gives himself over voluntarily into its hands.[61]

Schlier is correct to insist that the concept of Jesus' kingship expressed here is quite different from that ascribed to some later members of Jesus' family, who informed the emperor Domitian that his kingship was "heavenly" and would come only at the end of time.[62] Rather, as Josef Blank states, it is precisely the "unworldly" character of this kingship that allows it to call the political sphere into question as well.[63] Thus, when Pilate persists in asking whether Jesus claims to be a king, Jesus in typically Johannine fashion both acknowledges the use of the term and then transcends it by asserting that his real mission is to bear witness to the truth (18:37). Kingship, like other messianic conceptions in John, is thus admitted to the discussion but is redefined, not by denying its political nature but by stipulating how Jesus' kingship is realized and who his "subjects" are. Jesus is king as the witness who asserts the claim of God on the world, and his testimony achieves its consummation here before Pilate.[64] Jesus sets forth a universal challenge—"All who are of the truth hear my voice"—which confronts Pilate too but which Pilate declines. His refusal plainly implies that although Jesus, his servants, and his kingship are not of this world, Pilate and the king *he* serves most definitely are, and that the two must therefore inevitably come into conflict.

This impression is confirmed in the second dialogue between Jesus and Pilate (19:9–11). Here the silence of Jesus in response to Pilate's questions is part of the tradition,[65] but it has been given a characteristically Johannine transformation. For Pilate has asked Jesus what the world can never know, namely, "Where are you from?" (cf. 3:8; 7:27–28; 8:14; 9:29–30).[66] Receiving no answer, Pilate insists that his authority to release and to execute Jesus demands a reply. And now Jesus responds, in sharp language: "You would have no authority over me at all if it had not been given to you from above." The key term here is *anōthen,* "from above." It characterizes Pilate's authority *over Jesus* (not the state's authority in general!) as coming in fact from the same place as Jesus himself. The authority thus does not originate with Pilate or the world in which he governs, and Pilate's ignorance only confirms the fact that Jesus, as "from above," is totally superior to him (cf. 3:31). The Roman prefect's only power over the one who is "from above" is what God has granted in order that the world may work out its ignorance and hatred and the Son be glorified.[67] Indeed, it is just because of his powerlessness, his lack of competence in this matter (as in "truth"), that those who call God Father yet betray the Son have the greater sin (19:11).[68]

Thus in John's hands the idea that Rome's political authority comes "from above" has connotations very different from those it is usually thought to have in Romans 13. This authority is thoroughly relativized for the Johannine Christians, who, like Jesus, are themselves "from above" (John 3:3–8), are "not of this world," and therefore are hated and persecuted by the world (15:18–21; 16:1–4). There is here a clear refusal to acknowledge the authority of Rome, as a power limited to this world, over those who by believing in Jesus have become children of God and so gained the ascendancy over this world. Rome's power over them is limited to what God, their Father, may grant, and therefore is not Rome's power at all. Even Jesus' transcendence of the category of kingship is thus not "apolitical" (let alone apologetic), for the witness to truth confronts Caesar's man with a challenge beyond his grasp and in the end strips him of the authority he thinks is his.

Conclusion

Seen in the light of the political situation of Jews and Christians in the late first century, the treatment of political subjects in the Johannine narrative of Jesus' arrest and trial displays a twofold thrust. On the one hand, confrontation with Rome is not avoided. Rather, "what the trial suggests is that the disciple will always have to decide *vis à vis* the Empire whether Jesus is his king or whether Caesar is."[69] Roman soldiers participate in the arrest; they and only they beat and ridicule Jesus. It is a Roman official, not a Jewish court, who condemns him, despite claiming to find him innocent. The kingship of Caesar has a cruel advocate in Pilate, who spurns both the sovereignty of Israel and the royal witness to truth. Yet the Roman's hold on his authority is not so firm as he believes, for its source in this case is God, whose truth and whose rule he cannot comprehend. Being of this world, Rome has no authority of its own over those who are of God, and the witness to truth owes Rome nothing that Rome has the power to command. The "King of the Jews" thus represents precisely the fact that Israel can have no king but God, or the One sent by God, and he restores sovereignty to Israel by asserting the sovereignty of Israel's God over against all sovereignties of this world. "The Jews'" compliant acceptance of Caesar's claim to be their only king is bitterly denounced and is used to show that Pilate and they are at one in representing "the world." The rejection of Jesus as prophet, as revealer, as giver of life, is consummated in his rejection as King of the Jews.

On the other hand, it is exactly because the kingship of Jesus is not of this world that the confrontation between the two does not take place according to the standards of the world or according to its means. Jesus is contrasted not only with Caesar but also, albeit more lightly, with Barabbas, the *lēstēs,* the "freedom fighter." For John, freedom comes from knowing the truth, that is, from abiding in the word of Jesus (8:31–32). But this means the same thing as hearing the voice of the Good Shepherd, who lays down his life for the flock, not that of the hireling, much less the *lēstēs* (10:1–13).[70] It means abiding in the love of the one who lays down his life for his friends (15:9–17), hearing the voice of the king whose kingship is to testify to the truth (18:37) and whose enthronement is on the cross.[71] Only so can it be known who the followers of this king are (13:35). Telling the world the truth, then, is living in freedom. It is also living dangerously, but the conflict with the world's various dominions is not carried out or won on the world's terms. And yet it is won: *egō nenikēka ton kosmon,* "I have overcome the world," Jesus can say on the very verge of his betrayal (16:33).

The Fourth Gospel, for all its sectarianism and inwardness, does not offer a mere retreat from political relationships, though the approach to them that it does offer is every bit as radical as its radical Christology. Indeed, it is just the Johannine alienation from the world that ought to make John's refusal of allegiance to the world's political orders somewhat less than surprising. It was an alienation of consciousness as much as an overtly social one, to be sure, yet precisely as such it could be expected to be realized "in the world" as well. The politics of John may seem scarcely recognizable as politics to us. They may seem impractical or irresponsible in their stubborn devotion of all loyalty, political as well as spiritual, to Jesus who had been "raised up" as King of the Jews. But evidently for the Johannine Christians, who faced a complex and highly charged political situation, they were real politics and represented a real political option. The Fourth Gospel confronts the issue of Israel's freedom in the late first-century Roman Empire with an alternative to both zealotry and collaboration, by calling for adherence to the king who is not of this world, whose servants do not fight but remain in the world bearing witness to the truth before the rulers of both synagogue and Empire.

NOTES

1. Dodd, *Historical Tradition,* 213–215.

2. Ibid., 120, 216–217.

3. E.g., Dodd, ibid., 112; Ernst Haenchen, "Jesus vor Pilatus (Joh. 18, 28–29, 15)," in *Gott und Mensch,* by Ernst Haenchen, 149, 152; and Wayne A. Meeks, *The Prophet-King: Moses Traditions and the Johannine Christology,* 64, 76, 81. The pioneering work in this regard was done by Heinrich Schlier, "Jesus und Pilatus nach dem Johannes-evangelium," in *Die Zeit der Kirche* (4th ed.), by Heinrich Schlier, 56–74 (on the centrality of politics here, see, e.g., pp. 56–57, 61–64); and idem, "The State According to the New Testament," in *The Relevance of the New Testament,* by Heinrich Schlier, 215–225. In "Jesus und Pilatus" (originally published in 1941), Schlier explored the political implications of the course of Jesus' trial before Pilate in John; in "State" he developed his insights into a full-blown delineation of John's treatment of "the problem of the state" (pp. 224–225). The weakness in Schlier's work is this tendency to move toward a level of abstraction beyond John's real interests, in the course of which he seeks to distinguish between "the state" (Pilate) and "the world" (the Jews), with the *latter* seeking its salvation from "Caesar." This construction cannot be maintained exegetically, as will be seen below. Schlier's former teacher Rudolf Bultmann (*Gospel of John,* 633, 637, 651–663 passim) had made this same abstraction and distinction, though he drew less sweeping conclusions than Schlier.

4. E.g., Dodd, *Historical Tradition,* 115; Haenchen, "Jesus," 149–152; the commentaries of Brown (*Gospel According to John,* 2:868–869), Lindars (*Gospel of John,* 536), and E. C. Hoskyns and F. N. Davey (*The Fourth Gospel* [2d ed.], 521); and Anton Dauer, *Die Passionsgeschichte im Johannesevangelium,* 307–311.

5. Meeks stands nearly alone when he doubts that John's narrative could provide a model for Christians hoping to ward off a charge of sedition, since it calls for a decision between the kingship of Jesus and that of Caesar (*Prophet-King,* 64).

6. Morton Smith, "Palestinian Judaism in the First Century," in *Israel: Its Role in Civilization* (ed. Moshe Davis), 74–77.

7. Jacob Neusner, *From Politics to Piety: The Emergence of Pharisaic Judaism,* 143–154; and idem, *A Life of Yohanan ben Zakkai ca. 1–80 C.E.* (2d ed.), 166–173.

8. It is significant that *2 Baruch* looked for the punishment of Rome to be carried out by divine or messianic action rather than by Jewish military force (Frederick J. Murphy, "*2 Baruch* and the Romans," *JBL* 104 [1985] 663–669). Nevertheless, its author did hope for vengeance against the Romans and a deliverance from the status quo, and he believed that Jewish faithfulness was necessary to bring this deliverance about.

9. Emil Schürer, *The History of the Jewish People in the Age of Jesus Christ (175 B.C.–A.D. 135),* rev. ed. by Geza Vermes and Fergus Millar, 1:527.

10. Ibid., 529–533; and E. Mary Smallwood, *The Jews under Roman Rule,* 389–421.

11. Smallwood, *Jews under Roman Rule,* 421–427, 436–439; and Hugo Mantel, "The Causes of the Bar Kokba Revolt," *JQR* 58 (1968) 224–242, 274–296, esp. pp. 237–242.

12. So, in various ways, Dodd, *Historical Tradition,* 21–151, esp. p. 120 on the trial; Dauer, *Passionsgeschichte,* passim, esp. pp. 226–227, 334–336; Bultmann, *Gospel of John,* 641–644; and Brown, *Gospel According to John,* 2:787–791.

13. Both Schlier and Bultmann fell prey to this overabstraction (cf. n. 3 above); yet it was precisely the presence and the character of the actual German state of their time that elicited their reflections and gave them an unmistakable concreteness of their own.

14. Besides the commentaries, see especially Dauer, *Passionsgeschichte;* Josef Blank, "Die Verhandlung vor Pilatus Joh 18, 28–19, 16 im Lichte johanneischer Theologie," *BZ,* N.S. 3 (1959) 60–81; and Ignace de la Potterie, "Jésus roi et juge d'après Jn 19,13," *Bib* 41 (1960) 236–247.

15. Two other works, which I had not seen when this study first appeared in the *Journal of Biblical Literature,* support the essential literary and exegetical contentions here, though they do not draw conclusions regarding Johannine political thought. They are Duke, *Irony,* esp. pp. 126–137 on the trial narrative; and C. F. Evans, "The Passion of John," in C. F. Evans, *Explorations in Theology 2,* 50–66.

16. David R. Catchpole, in arguing against the presence of Roman troops at the actual historical arrest of Jesus (*The Trial of Jesus,* 148–151), denies that John intended the terms *speira,* "cohort," and *chiliarchos,* "tribune," to refer to Romans. But his evidence that these terms could refer to Jewish forces (p. 149) is not conclusive. Mentions of Jewish *chiliarchoi* and *speirai* (Judith 14:11; 1 Macc. 3:55; 2 Macc.

8:23; 12:20, 22; Josephus, *Antiquities* 17.9.3 §§215–216 and *Jewish War* 2.20.7 §§577–578; Mark 6:21) always refer to military units under the command of local sovereigns or leaders of rebellions, never to anything like what the Sanhedrin or the chief priests may have had available. In fact, John quite clearly distinguishes the *speira* from the *hypēretai*, "servants," of the "chief priests and the Pharisees," a fact that Catchpole cannot quite account for (pp. 150–151). John certainly meant that there were Romans in the Garden—which still does not prove there were any.

17. The presence of the tribune in 18:12 would seem to point to the entire cohort (Barrett, *Gospel According to St. John*, 518).

18. The decision about the traditionality and/or historicity of the Roman cohort is in fact very delicately balanced (cf., e.g., Dodd, *Historical Tradition*, 73–74, 118 n. 2). In favor of the cohort is the actual manner of Jesus' death; against it is the implausibility of several hundred Roman troops turning out, only to take Jesus to the *Jewish* authorities while failing to arrest the disciple who resisted (Catchpole, *Trial*, 150). Such implausibilities would hardly have deterred John from introducing the Romans on his own, and several commentators have been able to suggest motives for his doing so (e.g., Bultmann, *Gospel of John*, 633, 637; Barrett, *Gospel According to St. John*, 516, 518; and Schnackenburg, *Gospel According to St John*, 3:223; cf. Duke, *Irony*, 109). Yet in favor of their presence in pre-Johannine tradition is the fact that John lays no stress at all on their number or provenance (cf. Brown, *Gospel According to John*, 2:816). They are simply *there*, like the young man in Mark 14:51, and their very lack of definition is what makes them so puzzling.

19. See the discussion in chapter 2 above.

20. E.g., Bultmann, *Gospel of John*, 644, 646; Barrett, *Gospel According to St. John*, 523–524; and Schnackenburg, *Gospel According to St John*, 3:237. Schlier ("Jesus und Pilatus," 57; "State," 216) points out that the decision reached in the religious sphere must now find its realization in the political.

21. This is the common division found in, e.g., Brown, *Gospel According to John*, 2:858–859; Blank, "Verhandlung," 61; and Duke, *Irony*, 127. Evans ("Passion," 51) remarked that John's narrative is "the archetypal passion play."

22. Duke's very valuable study *Irony in the Fourth Gospel* brings this out clearly. Blank ("Verhandlung," 64–65) notes in relation to the role reversal by which Jesus the accused becomes accuser and judge that "in this situation nearly every word is paradoxical"; every event has a background that calls its foreground into question, and the exegete must be prepared to conceive of multiple, intersecting, or even contradictory references simultaneously.

23. Cf. Duke's remarks on the centrality of Pilate (*Irony*, 189 n. 23). In all of this, of course, no claims are being made about the "historical" Pilate but only about the character in John's story; and so for the others as well.

24. So the commentaries of Barrett (*Gospel According to St. John*, 531–546 passim), Brown (*Gospel According to John*, 2:863–864, 872, 885–896 passim), and Schnackenburg (*Gospel According to St John*, 3:241–267 passim); Blank, "Verhandlung," 73, 76, 80–81; Dodd, *Historical Tradition*, 96–97, 104–107, 119–120; Haenchen, "Jesus," 152–153; and Dauer, *Passionsgeschichte*, 308–310.

25. This is the particular position of Bultmann (*Gospel of John*, 655–665) and Schlier ("Jesus und Pilatus," 58–59, 65–73; and "State," 217–225), taken up to some extent by Blank ("Verhandlung," 71).

26. Barrett, *Gospel According to St. John*, 539.

27. E.g., Brown, *Gospel According to John*, 2:886–889; and Schlier, "Jesus und Pilatus," 67–68.

28. So also Duke, *Irony*, 128.

29. Haenchen, "Jesus," 150–151; and Dauer, *Passionsgeschichte*, 308.

30. This, of course, is the goal of the scene: Jesus must be crucified to fulfill his word (18:32), and Pilate must cooperate, willing or not; but his unwillingness seems slight indeed.

31. It is found in all four gospels; cf. Dodd, *Historical Tradition*, 99; and Bultmann, *Gospel of John*, 653–654. Note that in John, Jesus' "You say it" is used *twice* (18:34, 37).

32. Despite Haenchen ("Jesus," 151 n. 24), it is impossible not to hear the note of scorn in Pilate's question, even though this scorn does not by any means put Pilate on the side of Jesus. At the very least it is clear that Pilate distances himself from "the Jews" and their desire for a king.

33. Exegetes are rightly agreed that Pilate's question is not meant to express a philosophical skepticism but merely to identify him as not of the truth (e.g., Schnackenburg, *Gospel According to St John*, 3:251; and Brown, *Gospel According to John*, 2:869).

34. Meeks, *Prophet-King*, 63, 67.

35. Thus the endeavor by Bultmann (*Gospel of John*, 656) and Schlier ("State," 220, 224; contrast "Jesus und Pilatus," 65) to depict Pilate as representing a third force, "the state," attempting to remain neutral between accepting the truth and rejecting it in favor of the world, must be regarded as dubious. "What is truth?" expresses not neutrality toward but ignorance of truth.

36. Cf. Schnackenburg, *Gospel According to St John*, 3:251; and Brown, *Gospel According to John*, 2:871.

37. Barrett feels the difficulty of this (*Gospel According to St. John,* 539), while Bultmann, though recognizing Pilate's mockery, still speaks of his hope for "the Jews'" acquiescence (*Gospel of John,* 657).

38. Cf. Evans, "Passion," 59; Barrett, *Gospel According to St. John,* 539; and Lindars, *Gospel of John,* 563–564.

39. I.e., in the hope that they will regard this as punishment enough: so, e.g., Blank, "Verhandlung," 73; Schlier, "Jesus und Pilatus," 67–68; Bultmann, *Gospel of John,* 658; and Brown, *Gospel According to John,* 2:889.

40. Pilate certainly does not hope to arouse the sympathy of "the Jews" (so Haenchen, "Jesus," 153; and Schlier, "State," 222). Why would he expect that "the Jews," who want to have Jesus crucified, would feel sorry for him after only a scourging?

41. This theme has been worked out most convincingly by Blank ("Verhandlung," 62, 74–75); cf. de la Potterie (for 19:13–15), "Jésus," 236–240, 245–246; and Meeks, *Prophet-King,* 69–76.

42. Here the use of an insane man by the people of Alexandria to mock King Agrippa (Philo, *In Flaccum* 36–39) may be a relevant parallel. Commentators who take Pilate at his word often suppose that he means for "the Jews" to recognize Jesus' political harmlessness in his pathetic appearance (Bultmann, *Gospel of John,* 659; and Schnackenburg, *Gospel According to St John,* 3:256). But that *Jesus* could be humiliated would not have moved his enemies; they had brought him to Pilate for that very purpose. It is their *own* humiliation to which they react.

43. Cf. Schnackenburg, *Gospel According to St John,* 3:258. Pilate's third pronouncement of Jesus' innocence here serves merely to echo and recall with even sharper sarcasm the absurd second one in v. 4.

44. Several commentators (Bultmann, *Gospel of John,* 659; Brown, *Gospel According to John,* 2:877; and Dodd, *Historical Tradition,* 105 n. 1) see it as merely Pilate's sarcastic way of refusing "the Jews'" demand. This is plausible, and would be more so if we could take Pilate's declaration of innocence seriously; but the more often he repeats it, under these circumstances, the more hollow it rings.

45. Cf. Evans, "Passion," 60.

46. There seems little point in trying to see in *mallon* an indication that Pilate *must* have been afraid before, as several writers do (Bultmann, *Gospel of John,* 661; Blank, "Verhandlung," 77; and Schnackenburg, *Gospel According to St John,* 3:260, with n. 78). Nothing in his words or behavior to this point has suggested the slightest fear of either Jesus or the Jews.

47. So Barrett (*Gospel According to St. John,* 542) and Lindars (*Gospel of John,* 567); cf. Walter Bauer, William F. Arndt, and F. Wilbur Gingrich, *A Greek-English Lexicon of the New Testament,* s.v.

"*mallon*" 3a. The usage in John 5:18 (which Schnackenburg [n. 46 above] cites) should be carefully compared: there *mallon* seems to express precisely the *transition* from mere persecution for Sabbath-breaking (5:16) to the first efforts to kill Jesus for blasphemy.

48. The imperfect should be read as inchoative (cf. A. T. Robertson, *A Grammar of the Greek New Testament in the Light of Historical Research*, 885), not iterative (Schnackenburg, *Gospel According to St John*, 3:262) or conative (Brown, *Gospel According to John*, 2:879). Again John 5:18 is relevant: *dia touto oun mallon ezētoun auton . . . apokteinai*, "because of *this* they began rather to seek his death" (cf. n. 47 above).

49. De la Potterie has argued persuasively that John intends us to think of *Jesus* as being seated on the *bēma*, in line with his manifestation here as king and judge ("Jésus," 221–233).

50. To conceive of "the Jews" (or "the world") as standing in *contrast* to Pilate (or "the state") in putting all their hope in Caesar, as Schlier claims that John does ("State," 224–225), is to suggest a political impossibility for anyone in the late first century.

51. Cf., e.g., Bultmann, *Gospel of John*, 669; and Duke, *Irony*, 89.

52. De la Potterie, "Jésus," 244.

53. Meeks, *Prophet-King*, 76–78.

54. See Josephus, *Antiquities* 18.1.6 §23; and *Jewish War* 2.8.1 §118; 7.10.1 §410, 418.

55. Generally understood as abandoning their role as the messianic people, and so as God's people (e.g., Bultmann, *Gospel of John*, 665; and Brown, *Gospel According to John*, 2:894–895).

56. Cf. Meeks, *Prophet-King*, 76: "The political element in Jesus' kingship cannot be separated from its religious significance"; "the Jews," having rejected their eschatological king, cease to be God's special people and become instead merely one of Caesar's subject *ethnē*. So also Evans, "Passion," 61.

57. That John's *lēstēs* is meant to represent the same tradition about Barabbas as that found in the Synoptics is widely assumed (e.g., Bultmann, *Gospel of John*, 657–658; Brown, *Gospel According to John*, 2:872; and Blank, "Verhandlung," 73). Meeks proposes to connect the contrast between Jesus and Barabbas with John 10:1, 8, where the Good Shepherd is contrasted with *lēstai* (*Prophet-King*, 68). Oscar Cullmann (*Jesus and the Revolutionaries*, 36) sees in these *lēstai* of John 10 a reference to Zealot-style revolutionaries as false shepherds who led the sheep to slaughter.

58. So also Schlier, "State," 217–218; and Hoskyns and Davey, *Fourth Gospel*, 521.

59. Cf. Dauer, *Passionsgeschichte*, 308–309.

60. So also Evans, "Passion," 58–59.

61. "Das Zeugnis, das Jesus . . . ablegt, leugnet also nicht, dass er, Jesus, in dieser Welt einen Herrschaftsbereich habe. Es sagt freilich auch, dass dieses Reich seine Wurzeln nicht in dieser Welt habe. Damit stellt es freilich vor die Welt nur eine Herrschaft hin, die jede andere fundamental überragt. . . . Jesu Königreich erweist sich darin als nicht der Welt verhaftet, dass er, sein König, sich freiwillig in ihre Hände begibt" (Schlier, "Jesus und Pilatus," 62–63).

62. Ibid., 61–62, referring to Eusebius, *Historia ecclesiastica* 3.20.4. Cf. Meeks, *Prophet-King*, 64 n. 4.

63. Blank, "Verhandlung," 70.

64. Schlier, "Jesus und Pilatus," 63–64. In regard to messianic categories, Meeks notes that the function of the king is here redefined in terms of that of the prophet, with a reference to the Good Shepherd of John 10, whose sheep also "hear his voice" (*Prophet-King*, 66–67).

65. Cf. Dodd, *Historical Tradition*, 103–104; and Dauer, *Passionsgeschichte*, 118.

66. Cf. Schlier, "Jesus und Pilatus," 70; and Evans, "Passion," 60.

67. Cf. John 10:17–18; 13:31–32; 14:30–31; 15:22–25. Blank ("Verhandlung," 79) very acutely points out that Pilate's authority to act against Jesus is grounded, not in the nature of his authority itself, but in the plan of God; but to this authority, and to the freedom of the witness to truth, Pilate remains blind. Jesus' words do not in the first instance concern the authority and legitimacy of "the state" as such, but Pilate's authority *in this particular thing,* the case of Jesus: "The subject here is precisely not a theological foundation for the state's authority, but rather an indication of its limits" ("Es handelt sich hier gerade nicht um eine theologische Begründung staatlicher Autorität, sondern um eine Aufweis ihrer Grenze").

68. In the logic of the verse, this is preferable to explaining Pilate's lesser sin as due to his acting within a God-given political framework (Schlier, "Jesus und Pilatus," 71; and Bultmann, *Gospel of John,* 663); his relatively purer motivation (Brown, *Gospel According to John,* 2:893); or "the Jews'" having taken the first initiative (Bultmann, *Gospel of John,* 662).

69. Meeks, *Prophet-King*, 64. Cf. Evans, "Passion," 61: instead of Pilate offering "the Jews" a choice between Jesus and Barabbas, in 19:12 *they* offer *him* the choice between Christ and Caesar.

70. Cf. Meeks, *Prophet-King*, 68, 81; and nn. 57, 64 above.

71. Meeks, *Prophet-King, 68, 81;* see also de la Potterie, "Jésus," 246–247.

6
The Gospel of John and Liberation

I suggested in chapter 1 that, on the one hand, John's ideas about individual and group social relations tend to get relegated to a secondary level of concern in the interpretation of his gospel and that, on the other hand, the rise of a sociological approach to the New Testament is related to the movement of certain pressing social issues to the forefront of Christian theological discussion. The teaching and life of Jesus, the Synoptic gospels, and even the letters of Paul have already undergone a reexamination in some quarters to see what bearing they may have on these issues. This process may provide us with a stimulus (if not necessarily a justification) for putting similar questions to the gospel of John, especially in the context of the new understanding of that gospel that is now emerging.

My goal here, then, will be to relate certain concerns of the gospel of John to these social issues, which are often gathered together, perhaps somewhat uneasily, under the rubric of "liberation theology." After clarifying the terms in which such an investigation might take place, I shall take up two specific portions of the Johannine material with which we have already dealt—the figure of Nicodemus and the trial of Jesus—and examine what we have learned about them in the light of their significance for these issues. Finally, I shall turn to two broader areas of Johannine thought—namely, Christology and the ethic of love—and treat them in similar fashion.

I should say at the outset that I regard this undertaking as experimental and exploratory. Experiments can certainly fail and explorations can lead nowhere; but even so, the enterprise should at least make clear to us something of what is possible in this area, and perhaps something of what is impossible as well. Obviously we will not be looking at all the themes of liberation that could be considered in connection with John, and I do not claim that every theme in the Fourth Gospel has a direct bearing on liberation. Nor, for that matter, do I claim expert knowledge of liberation theology itself. I profess only a general awareness of its concerns, derived as much from subjective sympathies and personal experience as from any broad reading. Above all, I do not propose to set out in detail how liberation theologians ought to appropriate the gospel of John. That I must leave to the theologians themselves. My hope is that this study will be regarded as an offering from the realm of critical biblical scholarship of raw material only partially shaped, suggestions that may fertilize and give direction to the work of others.

Since definitions of the term "liberation theology" can vary widely, we will need to give at least some ad hoc precision to it in order that it may be useful in what follows. By "liberation theology" I mean, for present purposes, to refer to the theological assessment and undergirding of the liberation struggles of black people, women, the poor, and other oppressed groups, and of the struggle for peace among the world's nations. In so doing, I would deliberately include under this heading the widest possible range of black, Third World, feminist, and peace theologies. I do not regard a Marxist perspective as integral to liberation theology so defined. What is essential is a concern to relate both biblical texts and motifs and the themes of Christian theology in general to situations of oppression and violence and to the need and the means for their alleviation. In many cases this leads to a critique of biblical and Christian tradition as well as to a positive evaluation of them for the cause of liberation.

Whether or not this is a legitimate enterprise is more than we can undertake to demonstrate here. Readers who have already concluded that it is not will in all likelihood find little to persuade them otherwise. Nevertheless, while I do not propose to defend the whole enterprise that I have called liberation theology, it does seem necessary to examine at least some fundamental objections that might be raised specifically to its use of biblical texts.

One such objection is that this use forces upon the biblical writings a set of issues with which their authors were not and could not have been concerned. This is an especially serious problem for biblical criticism, which professes to seek out the meaning of the text itself in its original setting; and perhaps more than any other consideration, it gives biblical scholars legitimate reason to mistrust attempts to use the Bible as a document for liberation theology. But there are several factors that render this objection much less formidable than it might appear. In the first place, Christian theology (perhaps, indeed, every theology of a scriptural religion) has always put questions to its scriptures that extend far beyond the specific horizons of those scriptures' authors. Honest theologians always acknowledge this; and indeed there is precedent for it within the scriptures themselves. On any critical theory of relationships among the Synoptic gospels, later writers clearly did not hesitate to adapt the work of earlier ones to suit different conditions in theology, mission, and communal setting. As for John, the author himself declares quite frankly that the community's understanding of Jesus and his words changed radically in the time after his "glorification" (John 2:17, 22; 12:17; 14:25–26; 16:12–13).

For this very reason, to refuse to consider the bearing of the biblical text on the issues posed by liberation theology merely legitimates some other "forced" political interpretation of the text, namely, that of the traditional Christian theologies. For no theology by which any individual or church lives or has ever lived is without a social and political component, nor is there any reason to suppose that these components are any more closely related to "genuinely biblical" concerns than is liberation theology. It is idle to imagine otherwise; and it is equally idle to attempt to escape the dilemma by appealing to the supposedly apolitical interests of the biblical authors as a reason for constructing the political aspects of one's theology on some other basis altogether. That is simply to beg the question and to risk misreading the Bible as well. For if there is anything that the biblical God undeniably claims, it is the undivided loyalty of a faithful people; and if there is anything to this claim, then it is scarcely possible to rule any area of human concern out of bounds for the biblical writers. While these considerations are especially relevant within the Christian community, they ought to hold true even where biblical scholarship is pursued in a secular setting without relation to any explicit theological framework. In such a setting, there is certainly no call to impose the political outlook of traditional theology on the biblical text; and there should equally be no reason to deny that the biblical writers, in pursuing the claims that they did make (whether rightly or wrongly), took in a broader range of human life than what some forms of religion choose to call "religion."

It is not to be thought, of course, that we can find an articulated political philosophy in the gospel of 'ohn, or in the New Testament writers generally. But that, it seems to me, is beside the point. Does a theological concern to see justice and mercy done in the world depend on having a political philosophy? Or does it depend, as everything Christian depends, on the love of God and 'he word of God? No lack of systematic articulation, whether of an ancient or a modern kind, can prevent the text from turning the light of its claims about God onto any area of human endeavor. Nor can any imputation of dualistic or eschatological thought to early Christian writers and readers do so. That would be to grant authority over the real character of past events to mere heuristic devices. No one who believes that "eschatological" writing is ipso facto unconcerned with politics can have read much of it; and who is to say that a dualist *must* be uninterested in social or political matters? If John, at any rate, is a dualist, I think it has been adequately shown before this writing that he is far from being "otherworldly" in matters of social relationship.

It may still be objected that to address, not political concerns in general, but the cause (or causes) of liberation in particular, to biblical texts is inevitably to force on these texts an agenda that is not their own, to make them a mere sounding board for positions that originate and are given their really decisive formation elsewhere. To the extent that this objection has not already been met in the foregoing discussion, it can be overcome only by substantiating the claim that there are biblical texts that treat situations of oppression comparable to those treated by liberation theology and that they do so in a relevant fashion. Precisely this is the point that I want to make about John, that at least some of the interests of liberation theology are in fact integral to this gospel, because it emanates from what may with reason be called an oppressed community.

In many ways the gospel of John seems the least promising of all the gospels for a theology of liberation. There is, to begin with, its remoteness from the historical Jesus. We find here none of Jesus' radical social and economic pronouncements, little of his solidarity with the poor and the outcast. John's focus instead is on Christology itself, with an almost tedious insistence. We have seen, to be sure, that John's Christology is by no means unrelated to social and even political issues. Even so, however, the inwardness of the "spiritual gospel" has generally seemed to imply an individualism that would offer little light on the specific issues addressed by liberation theology. Hence we find that John has been for the most part (though not entirely) left out of account in the discussion of these issues.

The social approach to John and the new understanding that it brings us may alter this situation, and that is a significant part of its revolutionary import. For it is now both possible and necessary, I would contend, to view the gospel of John as the product of an oppressed community and to draw further conclusions on that basis. It is important, however, to be very careful and very clear in understanding what exactly is meant by "oppression" here. While we know almost nothing about the social class background of the Johannine community, it is probably true that this community was not economically or politically oppressed, at least not any more than were other Jews and religious fringe groups in the Roman Empire. That is to say, they will have been, like other Christians, subject to only sporadic persecution by government officials, as a nonconforming religion cut off from the protection Rome gave to the tolerated nonconformity of Judaism. As we have seen, they retained a form of the anti-Roman Jewish messianism that was by no means restricted to Palestine. Far more significant, however, was the group's fundamental sense of deracination, of a disenfranchisement and alienation imposed on them forcibly by those who had been their own people. This sense resulted from the conflicts that led up to, and continued after, their expulsion from the synagogue. At any rate, there is no question that the Johannine group *saw themselves* as oppressed. They heard Jesus saying to them, "If the world hates you, know that it has hated me before you. . . . If they persecuted me, they will persecute you too. . . . Indeed, the hour is coming when everyone who kills you will suppose he is offering a service to God" (John 15:18, 20b; 16:2b).

We have in John, then, a situation of oppression that is partially, though only partially, analogous to the conditions addressed by liberation theology. Because the analogy is only a partial one, it may be that there are oppressive situations today to which John cannot speak or in which what it has to say may be of only limited relevance. I do not wish to exaggerate the claims that can be made about the Fourth Gospel; and in the end it must be those who are actually engaged in the theological analysis of any particular situation who judge the relevance or irrelevance of John to that situation. Nevertheless, it is my claim that, in the light of our new understanding, the elements in John analogous to contemporary oppression not only may but must be sought out and evaluated.

My intention here is to unfold these elements in the Fourth Gospel, to ask how the response of the Johannine Christian community to its perceived oppression may be relevant to the search for a Christian response to oppression today. Let me stress once again that this undertaking should be seen as an experiment and that I do not claim that everything in John is relevant in this way or must be interpreted in this light. Yet the possibility and the demand to interpret *some* things in this way seem inescapable. In the process we will look not only for prescription, for authoritative theological guidance from John regarding liberation, but also for simple description, for patterns in the Johannine response to oppression whose significance would then remain to be determined. It is quite possible that some of these patterns will turn out to give negative guidance, for, as we shall see, there are dangers inherent in the Johannine way.

Ours is not the first effort that has been made along these lines.[1] More than a dozen years ago Frederick Herzog published *Liberation Theology,* a study of "liberation in the light of the Fourth Gospel."

The title suggests an exciting premise; but on the whole the book proves to be a disappointment. It is in fact "an attempt to develop an outline of Christian theology" in which "the Fourth Gospel text merely stakes out the area in which [Herzog is] attempting to identify present theological priorities."[2] Sometimes the text does not seem to play even that prominent a role, and the neglect of exegesis means that we seldom get to hear what *John* has to say about liberation, only what Herzog believes *must* be said about it, connected somehow to the Johannine text. This is not to say that Herzog's work is without value, only that exegetical weakness and a too rapid transposition of John's message into terms of "selfhood," "unconcealment," and the like all too often leave us unable to say exactly what John's contribution to the subject is.

Such is not the case with José Porfirio Miranda's *Being and the Messiah.* This remarkable book manages to make significant contributions both to existentialist and liberation theology and to biblical criticism. Miranda makes two fundamental assertions: that the absolute imperative—that is to say, God—exists only in the outcry of the other, the neighbor in need; and that time is real, that is, that reality consists not in the unchanging, timeless truths of Platonist philosophy but in the contingency and changefulness of passing time.[3] On this basis, he insists that biblical eschatology be taken seriously, that is, that the kingdom of God is a real, perceivable change in the circumstances of this world, that it is a change in favor of justice for the needy—and that it *has come* in Jesus the Messiah.[4] That John makes *this* claim about Jesus is what makes his message a liberative one, the more so since he relates the acceptance or rejection of this claim to the doing of "good works," a term that Miranda interprets to mean "the doing of good to the needy."[5] John's message, according to Miranda, is that God is revealed in Jesus precisely in his doing of these "good works," so that God is known precisely and only in the keeping of the word, the commandment, of love for the neighbor.[6]

We will have cause to refer to Miranda's work again later in this chapter. Here I may say that he seems absolutely correct in his assertion that for John the messianic event, that which overthrows the world, has broken into the world as *fact* and unleashed the world's hostility.[7] This is nothing more than John's well-known "realized eschatology." Usually, however, this eschatology is discussed in terms of individual faith and "eternal life." Miranda suggests, rather, that John's concern is with eschatological *community* and that this is what must be addressed. Because it does not take into account the developments in Johannine studies outlined in chapter 1 above, Miranda's study is missing what I hope to show is a powerful exegetical tool in this regard. Miranda may also overestimate the extent to which John spells out in precise social terms the threat felt by the world in Jesus' messiahship, while underestimating the extent to which the Fourth Gospel is a closed system, so that even the Johannine epistles (let alone the Synoptic gospels) are of limited comparative usefulness. Therefore the parallels used to define "good works" are not absolutely demonstrative. Nevertheless, Miranda's book is one of the most exciting and challenging works on John to appear in recent years, and even exegetes who disagree with him will be unwise not to respond to him.

Thus while some groundwork has been laid, there remains much room for experimentation in testing how, if at all, the gospel of John can be significant for the theology of liberation, as for other issues confronting contemporary Christianity. We will begin our exploration of this subject by considering again some of the Johannine material we have treated in earlier chapters.

Solidarity with the Oppressed: Nicodemus

In previous chapters we have seen that Nicodemus represents a specific group in the social environment of Johannine Christianity, namely, the "secret Christians." These were people, some of them evidently in positions of authority, who held a form of Christian faith, but not the exalted Johannine Christology, and who sought an accommodation between Christianity and the synagogue. To do this, in the Johannine situation, they had necessarily to conceal their belief in Jesus lest they be expelled from the synagogue community. Their low Christology and lack of open discipleship caused John to regard them as still in need of birth from above, the birth from water and spirit that is urged on Nicodemus in John 3. To be born from *water* and spirit means, for John, to adhere to the group of those who fully acknowledge Jesus and to begin a new life, having a new birth, with them. Just this adherence was what the secret disciples represented by Nicodemus sought to avoid in any open way. The new birth that was demanded of them thus implied not only personal faith and sacramental initiation but a change of social location as well.[8] They must not only accept Jesus but also declare their acceptance by openly joining the community of his disciples. This is what baptism stands for in John 3, a dangerous social relocation, a choosing of sides at the border between a familiar and secure social setting and the disenfranchised Johannine community.

In this relocation the birth from spirit and the birth from water are inseparable: they are *one* birth, from water and spirit. The divinely given gift of new life and the change of social location come as an indivisible whole; indeed, it is precisely the attempt to divide them that ruins Nicodemus. To be born from God through faith in Jesus

Christ—simply put, to be a Christian—is, for John, to have an altered relationship both to God and to other people, a new identity that is both spiritual and social; i.e., that is fully human. Neither aspect is subordinated to the other; in fact, the two cannot rightly be distinguished.

This is to say that Johannine faith means adherence to the *community* of faith. It is not the holding of a merely private opinion, one that, even if it is shared by others, is still best expressed alone and in the dark. It is not merely a personal transaction between the believer and God, though it is certainly that as well. What Nicodemus stands in need of is not just a conviction, not just a transformed inner life, and certainly not just a rite or a sacrament. He needs a transfer, a joining. Nicodemus is challenged to join the action of God in the unfamiliar and the improbable. To be born of God is to be born into a people, and (from Nicodemus' point of view) into the most improbable people, the rabble who know not the law, the radicals, the fanatics.

Thus what the gospel of John calls for on the part of the secret Christians is a public transfer of allegiance. This is what Nicodemus successfully avoids in the council of the Pharisees and rulers in John 7, as we saw, and it is this avoidance which is criticized so sharply in John 12:42–43. In these passages, but especially in John 3, the Fourth Evangelist seems to appeal to the secret Christians in high places to make an open confession and take their stand with the oppressed community. We should not underestimate the risk he is calling on them to take. They are being asked to jeopardize their position as rulers and their standing as Pharisees, to align themselves with the "accursed" (7:49).[9] They are being asked, in fact, to switch sides from persecutor to persecuted. The group they are being asked to join has no status, no power, no place in the world. They are being asked to dislocate and displace themselves socially, to undertake an act of deliberate downward mobility. Quite possibly they are being asked to risk their lives. That is what John wants of them, concretely, when he says to them, "You must be born from above."

Herzog translates this expression as "You must *become black*" and speaks of "being enabled to identify with . . . the people on the borders of society," ceasing to "go into hiding" and instead joining the "new corporateness [in which] the new life is experienced."[10] In this he has very accurately seen the essence of John 3. Nicodemus—that is, the group of people in the late first century whom he symbolizes— is being called upon to leave a secure, if ambivalent, situation by making known his solidarity with an oppressed minority. He is bidden to *decide,* and is told that on one side, and on one side only, lies the eternal life of God. He is told to come out of hiding.

That is not what the comfortable person in any society wants.

Particularly in the West, ambivalence and ambiguity have very nearly been canonized as the inevitable condition, if not indeed the ultimate aspiration, of modern humanity, in ethics, aesthetics, politics, and religion. We are constantly being reminded that there are no absolutes, no easy choices. I would feel much more comfortable about sharing this perception if it were clear that we who promote it are entirely disinterested; but we are not, for it is what enables us to hide. John would agree that there are no *easy* choices. His point, though, is that there are choices.

The choice that faced Nicodemus was whether or not to side, no longer in private but openly, with a specific oppressed group in his society—indeed, with those whom the members of his own rank and class, the people whose company he truly preferred, were oppressing. The situation is complicated, of course, by Nicodemus' secretly espoused sympathy with the persecuted group in question. He was, in his own mind, perhaps already one of them, though unwilling to have it made known. This means that analogies to other situations of oppression must be drawn with the greatest care. It is not really possible for a white person to become black, and only with great difficulty can a rich person become poor. Yet even openly expressed sympathy has its dangers. In an oppressive society the fate of the "kaffir-boete," the "nigger-lover," the "fellow-traveler" is only too well known.

Having stretched our theological vocabulary to this extent, can we speak more precisely still? Where is Nicodemus to be found today? This especially we would prefer to leave ambiguous; but I will try, with all due caution, to name some names. Nicodemus is to be found, to begin with the most exact analogy, where Christians in power relate to powerless Christians. This is true whether power is derived from money, class, gender, race, education, political connection, or otherwise. It applies to white Christians in relation to blacks in the United States and in South Africa. It applies to affluent members of church hierarchies in relation to peasants and the poor, in Latin America but certainly not only there. It applies to men in relation to women in nearly all societies. It applies to the educated in relation to the ignorant, the well fed in relation to the hungry, the healthy in relation to the sick. I would say, too, that it applies to the born in relation to the unborn, present humanity in relation to the future that is powerless to prevent our crimes against it. Certainly it applies to any Christian who has not let this identity be known in a place where real danger might result. This includes those who are reluctant to become known as activists in struggles for justice and for peace, since, as we shall see more fully below, for John the one way in which Christians are known is by their love for one another.

I have tried to name my own name as often as possible in the foregoing list; but in fact the making of lists is not the task at hand. In essence, Nicodemus is to be found wherever one whose life is secure must face those whose life is insecure, or who struggle in the cause of God, and decide to say, "I am one of them." Only by this decision and this declaration can Nicodemus avoid complicity in their oppression. But only so does he also find his own new birth, the gift of new identity, both spiritual and social, that comes from an allegiance to God, and the one whom God sent, that is publicly given. Nicodemus is most likely to show up somewhere in the dead of night. When he does, he must hear of the kingdom of God. But he must also hear—*we* must hear, when we find, as we inevitably shall, that it is we who are Nicodemus—that a transformation is involved, one that comes from God but transpires before the world and shapes a new identity: "You must be born again."

Jesus and Caesar

In chapter 5 above, I defined John's political stance as allegiance to the kingship of Jesus, which he presents as a third alternative to the claims of both Caesar and the Zealots. Rome is seen as hostile to the hope of oppressed Israel, but Rome's authority is undermined and relativized by the assertion of God's sovereignty in the kingship of Jesus. Israel's true allegiance must be to God, not Caesar, and for John this allegiance is now fittingly expressed in adherence to Jesus the King. The authority of Rome over those who adhere to him is dissolved, for they are now, as he is, "from above," and Rome's only power over them, as over him, is what God may choose to grant. Jewish acceptance of the claims of Caesar is therefore also condemned. On the other hand, if Jesus is the king by whom God's sovereignty is asserted, then Israel may look for no other, and John likewise rejects the desire for a violent revolutionary like Barabbas. Jesus' kingship will inevitably come into conflict with the kingships of this world, but precisely because it is "not of this world," the conflict is not carried out on the world's terms. Jesus' followers do not fight, and his enthronement is on the cross. The sovereignty that Jesus asserts against Caesar is that of Israel's God, but precisely as *God's* sovereignty and not the world's it is not won by violence.

Thus for John, Jesus is king as the witness to truth who confronts the world with the claim of God and the love of God.[11] He asserts the sovereignty of God against the world's sovereignties but also against the claims of those who would overthrow those sovereignties with violence. His kingship, moreover, is for the oppressed community with whom he is one and whose allegiance now no longer belongs to the world's kingships. Just this alienation of allegiance is seen by the world as subversive and draws down its hatred in response.

What do John's politics imply for liberation? Above all, they offer hope to those oppressed by the sovereignties of this world by offering them instead the sovereignty of God. What is involved is first of all a revolution of consciousness, the alienation of their allegiance away from the idolatrous and oppressive orders of the world toward the truth of God, the truth that makes free. For John, God the creator is by no means the sustainer of the world's religions, states, and economies. Rather, when God the Logos, through whom the world was made, entered the world, the world "knew him not" and refused the light precisely because its works were evil (John 1:10–11; 3:16–21).[12] The victims of these evil works, of the world's whole vast machinery of avarice and harm, may welcome the light for the very reason that the world abhors it. It is those who "do the truth" who come to the light, and it is by knowing the truth that the world itself could be set free from its sin. Jesus liberates by speaking his word, which is true and is truth, just as his kingship means his testimony to the truth (8:31–47; 17:17; 18:37). This "truth" is the reality of God and of God's claim upon the world, expressed and acknowledged in love for one another against the oppressive hatred in the world. Allegiance to God's sovereignty through Jesus the King subverts the orders of the world, and only this subverts them truly.

John thus calls for a questioning and even a withdrawal of allegiance from the world's orders, not because order is wrong, but because the *world's* orders have forgotten God, however much they may claim to know God.[13] Jesus and Caesar cannot both be king; those who choose the sovereignty of God cannot, as far as John is concerned, give allegiance to the world as well. Because they are under God's sovereignty, moreover, the world's power over them is broken, and the hold it may still think it has on them is an illusion (19:11). But by the same token, no new order erected and maintained by the world's means can represent Jesus' kingship either. John sets us free to question and to criticize revolutionary orders as well, if they also become one of the world's allegiances and so carry on the world's oppression rather than ending it.

It might well be asked whether John's absolutism here is not a result of the Johannine community's unique historical circumstances, so that in fact some particular state or order could conceivably embody the kingship of Jesus acceptably. This is not at all beyond imagination, since every Christian vision of society is precisely an attempt to imagine it. But such an order would have to be an order of love and an order of the cross, and we must admit that, whatever is conceivable, no state and no institution, not even the church itself, has *in reality* been this. Yet the very elusiveness of the kingship of Jesus would provoke a truly Johannine Christianity not to despair but to renewed effort at realizing it in the Christian community and to renewed resistance against the claims of worldly orders to absolute allegiance.

The community of Jesus the King will, like Jesus, bear witness in the world to the truth and offer the world the sovereignty of God against its own oppression. In so doing, they will draw this oppression down upon themselves; for John, the inscription "King of the Jews" can hang only on the cross. But it is in this community, where the word of love is kept, that the sovereignty of God is truly known and made known, and it is by this knowledge that the oppressed are empowered to deny their oppressors' right. The first step in liberation is the liberation of consciousness, stripping the oppressor of the claim to right and authority over the lives of the oppressed and opening up the possibility of a new allegiance. Only so can people be freed to imagine their own liberation, once they have conceived of an order other than what is and a rule other than oppression. The kingship of Jesus represents a perpetual liberation of awareness and subversion of allegiance away from the orders of oppression.

"Anyone who makes himself a king is defying Caesar" (John 19:12). By refusing to grant allegiance to Caesar or to acknowledge his authority, Johannine Christianity provides the fundamental prerequisite for undermining his rule. By giving allegiance instead to Jesus as King, it lays the groundwork for an ongoing nonviolent resistance to every nationalism, every oppression, and every ideology that would play the role of Caesar. In this way John makes justice possible, by removing from injustice the aura of sovereignty with which it surrounds itself and by pointing the way toward freedom in the truth of the sovereignty of God.

Johannine Christology and a Jesus for the Oppressed

Liberation Christology has in general appealed strongly to the Jesus of history, or at any rate to the Synoptic Jesus, for its subject matter. It speaks of the Jesus who ministered to the oppressed and proclaimed God's kingdom in their favor, and who died as one of them as the result of his clash with the established structures of power.[14] But this Jesus, apart perhaps from the conflict with power, is evidently not the Johannine Jesus, and the Christology of John in all its distinctiveness has had relatively little impact on the discussion of Jesus the liberator. John presents us with an otherworldly Christ, a divine figure who seems to be of no relevance to the social and political struggles of oppressed people. What I hope to demonstrate here is that this Johannine Jesus is not, after all, out of touch with the oppressed. By examining the relationship between Jesus and the oppressed community in John, I hope to discover some suggestive features of Johannine Christology that can then be fruitfully compared with the way Christology has functioned particularly within black theology and black Christianity.

In what must now be regarded as a seminal work, Wayne Meeks proposed in 1972 to study the meaning of Johannine christological symbolism not as "a chapter in the history of ideas" but in its functioning within the Johannine community.[15] He explored the way in which John typically portrays Jesus as an alien, a stranger, John's insistence that Jesus is "from above," "from heaven," "not of this world." As a result, Jesus is incomprehensible to the world, while the world refuses to hear what he has to say. In symbolic language, Jesus "comes down" from heaven and "goes up" again there, but those who are "of this world" understand nothing about him. Thus the Johannine claim that Jesus descended from above expresses not the union of heaven and earth but their estrangement.[16] But, as Meeks pointed out, this estrangement represents also the alienation of the Johannine community. In the course of the gospel, John depicts Jesus' progressive alienation from "the Jews," while at the same time depicting the disciples' similar detachment from them and attachment to Jesus. Thus in John the history of the disciples and the history of Jesus himself, in their ever-increasing alienation from Judaism and "the world," symbolize the history of the Johannine community. Their rejection and deracination are figured in that of Jesus.[17] John's high Christology thus reinforces the community's social identity, that is to say, its deprivation of identity and formation of a new identity. We can discern in this process a dialectic between the growth of high Christology and the community's disenfranchisement. It was, after all, their christological confession that apparently led to their expulsion from the synagogue. As this alienation grew, the development of a still higher Christology both expressed and compensated for their sense of loss; but the higher their Christology became, the greater grew the rift between them and synagogue Judaism.[18] The otherworldly, exalted Christ of the Fourth Gospel is thus directly related to the communal experience of the Christians for whom it was written.[19]

Another aspect of John's Christology may also be noted here. This is the way in which all religious functions and symbols tend to be concentrated in Jesus in the Fourth Gospel. In common with early Christianity in general, John holds that the Jewish scriptures bear witness to Jesus (5:39). It is a step beyond this when he apparently sees in Jesus the fulfillment and in some sense the transcendent replacement of the feasts and observances of Judaism, such as Passover: Jesus is killed at the same time as the Passover lambs, and, like them, no bone of his is broken (19:14, 36). Likewise he transcends the manna of the exodus (6:32–35, 48–51). Other symbols, found in the scriptures but also common in Jewish (and non-Jewish) religion in John's day, find their fulfillment in the Johannine Jesus too: he is the Bread, the Water, the Light, the Shepherd. Moreover, specifically Jewish eschatological hopes are entirely "localized" in Jesus: he is Messiah, Prophet, and King; but he is also the Resurrection itself, and he is Life (11:25). The list could be extended; ultimately Jesus is the way through whom all must come to the Father (14:6), and Thomas finally confesses him as both Lord and God (20:28). In the concrete situation of the Johannine community, this means that, forcibly cut off from their religious heritage, they have concentrated that heritage, its observances and its hopes, entirely in the figure of Jesus. By these means the Fourth Evangelist hopes that they will overcome their fear of disenfranchisement, confident that in Jesus they have all that their enemies mean to deny them, and more.[20]

Let us summarize these findings and elaborate on them a bit further. The essential point is that the Johannine community found the alienation and the oppression that they experienced symbolized in the figure of Jesus. Their Jesus tradition was thus interpreted in the light of this experience. Their worship of Jesus as divine both contributed to their estrangement from Judaism and became the vehicle for expressing that estrangement. In the rejection of Jesus by the world that could not know him they portrayed their own rejection. In Jesus who was before all things they concentrated their own lost religious heritage.

An inevitable concomitant of this process is the solidarity between Jesus and the oppressed community that is expressed in such a variety of ways in the Fourth Gospel. Jesus and the Christians share the world's rejection and hostility. This is sometimes explicitly stated, as in the words of John 15:18 ("If the world hates you, know that it has hated me before you"), or in the reference to Jesus' death in John 12:26 ("If anyone serves me, let that person follow me; and where I am, there will my servant be also"). At other times Jesus simply speaks in the plural, as in John 3:11 ("We speak of what we know and testify to what we have seen, and you people do not accept our testimony"). One in their rejection by the world, Jesus and the community are also one in their origin; for the Christians too are born "not of the will of a man, but of God" (1:13) and are "not of this world" (17:14, 16). Thus the seemingly arrogant Johannine claim that Jesus came down from heaven (6:42) applies in effect to the Johannine Christians themselves, though Marinus de Jonge points out that they are God's children only in dependence on Jesus; they are not "sons" as he is "the Son."[21] Also like Jesus, they are sent into the world and bear witness in it (15:27;

17:18; 20:21). Ultimately, their hope is the same as their danger, that where he is, there they will be also (14:3; 17:24).

Jesus thus becomes the matrix for the community's life and self-awareness. It defines itself and its relation to the world of its oppressors in terms of him—that is, on its own terms, not the world's. Its relation to the holy, to the sacred world and to God, is likewise expressed in terms of Jesus. So is its desire for internal unity: they wish to be one, as Jesus and the Father are one (17:21–23). The ultimate grounding of the assurance that enables them to persevere in the face of the world's hostility is also in Jesus: "In the world you have trouble; but courage! I have overcome the world!" (16:33).

How may we relate this functional understanding of John's Christology to the Christology of oppressed peoples, and particularly to black Christology? The Johannine community differed from black Christianity in one important respect, namely, in that it was oppressed precisely *because* of its Christology. Nevertheless it is possible to make some suggestions, and I hope that others will be able to take the hints given here and develop them much further.

The late Benjamin Mays in his book *The Negro's God* distinguished two basic patterns of talk about God in black religious writing. One of these, the compensatory, presents God as offering comfort in the troubles of this unjust world and appropriate compensation to oppressed and oppressor in the next, without much thought of a change of circumstances here and now. The other pattern draws on traditional ideas of God's love, justice, and impartiality to urge blacks to struggle against oppressive conditions and work to establish social righteousness.[22] Similar patterns could no doubt be observed, *mutatis mutandis,* in black thought about Jesus. Of these two patterns, it is obviously the second to which black theology has largely appealed in its presentation of Jesus as liberator.

James Cone, however, in his *God of the Oppressed,* seems to move toward a coalescence of the two motifs, in the sense that he finds liberative value in the first, "compensatory" pattern as well. For Cone, the comforting presence of Jesus experienced by black Christians under oppression enabled not only endurance and hope for another world but validation and struggle in this one. In the experience of Jesus' presence, Cone writes, "They realized that he bestowed a meaning upon their lives that could not be taken away by white folks." This presence affirmed black humanity and human value, in contravention of the dehumanizing experience of white oppression.[23] In Cone's words, Jesus "was their truth, enabling them to know that white definitions of black humanity were lies. . . . Jesus Christ was that reality who invaded their history from beyond and bestowed upon them a definition of humanity that could not be destroyed by the whip and the pistol." Jesus thus became the basis for a new way of looking at reality, enabling a struggle against oppression.[24] This *presence* of Jesus forms an indispensable part of black christological understanding, according to Cone, a present activity that is to be related to the past activity of the "historical Jesus."[25] This "contemporization" of Jesus, if we may call it that, is similarly seen in the identification of the suffering of Jesus with that of black people.[26]

I believe there are evident parallels in this to the functioning of Christology in John. The "contemporization" of Jesus—the reexperiencing of his past in the present of an oppressed community—is the very warp on which the "seamless robe" of the Fourth Gospel is woven. More than any other gospel, John offers an understanding of Jesus produced by reflection on his past in the light of his present activity.[27] And the result of this understanding is to provide location and validation to a community disenfranchised by the "world" and its authorities. For John's community as for black Christians, the world is wrong because Jesus is right. They are not what the world says they are; their true identity is to be found in the presence of Jesus. Their alienation from the oppressor's world does not mean what the oppressor thinks it means, because Jesus himself experienced that same alienation. In a profoundly true sense, for the Johannine Jesus to say, "They are not of the world just as I am not of the world," means the same thing as for James Cone to say that Jesus is black. In both cases, a community's worth is affirmed against the denial of it by an oppressor through the group's knowledge of Jesus, both past and present. Likewise, the oppressed are assured that God stands with them, despite the strength and self-assurance of the world, and so they are enabled to withstand the world and resist its oppression. The presence of the Father and the Son in the gospel of John enables both endurance and witness against the world (the whole tenor of the Farewell Discourses in John 14–17). That is to say, it enables struggle, in whatever way is possible at a given time and is consistent with the word of Jesus, analogously to what Cone affirms about the black community. When Cone also says that "Jesus Christ is . . . the content of the hopes and dreams of black people,"[28] he opens up a fruitful avenue for exploration regarding the similar way in which the Johannine Jesus focuses all the sacred hopes and symbols of the community.

From this comparison I hope we may have gained some new insights into both the Fourth Gospel itself and some ways in which it can be fruitful for liberation theology. Here is a biblical model of an oppressed community claiming its validity, courage, and hope through Jesus Christ. Yet the Johannine affirmation of Jesus is not without its dangers, and these too must be given at least some brief treatment here. For in the famous phrase of Ernst Käsemann, there may be a "naive docetism" inherent in John's Christology, with its Jesus who is not of this world and who seems so much more divine than human.[29] In John's case, this is because it is precisely the divinity of Jesus which it is the gospel's main purpose to affirm in the context of the struggle with the synagogue. But is there not a similar danger in the Christology of the God-Man, the superhuman King Jesus, that sometimes comes to expression in black Christianity?

There are certainly positive factors in such a Christology. The eternity and the power of a Jesus so conceived are able to fortify the community and its members against the precariousness and uncertainty of their own continued existence: he, at least, will always be there. The triumph of this Jesus over pain and suffering, his invulnerability, can furnish a vision that enables the people, in their turn, to endure. The Jesus of the gospel song "I'll Rise Again," who is so unconcerned at having nails driven into his hands, is surely very Johannine (cf. John 10:17–18; 19:25–30)—and very docetic. But the point of the docetic conception is the singer's identification with Jesus and his triumph over rejection and oppression.

The danger in this, however, is that it leads all too easily to an otherworldliness that is merely escapist. The world and its history, including its pain, become simply unreal, and the believer is encouraged to avoid dealing with them rather than turn to God for their transformation. Something similar apparently happened in the Johannine community, for the First Epistle of John seems to have been written precisely to condemn a docetic interpretation of Johannine Christology, one that turned away both from the physicality of Jesus and from the concrete deeds of love which alone can realize his messiahship.[30] Even where overt doctrinal docetism is not present, Christianity must always beware of any ultra-Johannine conception of Jesus that removes him from the human world of pain and joy and doubt, and makes him into a superman who—paradoxically enough —is subject to our bidding and confirms our self-centeredness. When John's overwhelming emphasis on the divinity of Jesus and his supremacy over the world remains linked to the validation of the oppressed over against the contempt of their oppressors, it serves a significant part of its original purpose. When it is used to present the oppressed with a means of giving up on the world and so absconding from it, then it is misused. A worse misuse yet occurs when the oppressors themselves take up this all-powerful Jesus and claim to rule in his name, justifying their power as an extension of his, allowing Jesus to rule in the other world so long as they can rule in this one, and leaving the oppressed only the hope that—if they are good—they will visit him there.

The Johannine Love Ethic and Liberation

There is an ancient legend according to which the apostle John in extreme old age said nothing except to murmur over and over again, "My little children, love one another" (Jerome, *Commentary on Galatians* 6.10). And so most people today, if asked to characterize the ethics of John's gospel, would no doubt call it the gospel of love.

The theme of love that pervades the Johannine Farewell Discourses exemplifies in a peculiar way the relation of the Fourth Gospel to the historical Jesus, both the faithfulness and profundity of its insight into him and the vast difference that separates it from him. With a purity of focus unmatched in any of the Synoptics, John has seen the essence of Jesus' ethical intention in the single commandment, "Love"; yet he reduces the scope of this commandment in a way that all but undermines the intention of the historical Jesus, making it read, "Love *one another*." Not "your enemies"; not even "your neighbor as yourself"; but only "one another." The commandment is directed to Jesus' followers; the love is to be something that is among themselves, and precisely as such is to be a sign that they *are* his followers (13:34–35).[31] Here, then, is the sublimity of Johannine Christianity, and here also is its perilous flaw. For beautiful as such a restricted love may appear from within the Christian community, it may seem far less attractive from the outside. It is the implications of this love and of its restriction that I want to explore here, in the light of liberation.

For the Synoptic Jesus (and the same is probably true of the historical Jesus), the injunction to love is occasioned by the love of God for all, even the unrighteous (Luke 6:35–36 // Matt. 5:44–45). In John, it is based on the love of Jesus for the disciples (13:34; 15:12) and ultimately on the love of God for Jesus (17:26). Thus the limitation of the love commandment corresponds to a characteristic Johannine limitation of the scope of God's concern: it is for the disciples, but not for the world (cf. 14:22–24; 17:9).[32] This is related to the issue of sectarianism in the Fourth Gospel. As we saw in chapter 1, it seems impossible to avoid characterizing the Johannine community as a "sect," at least in terms of its relations with Judaism. The point to be made here is that such a group may have attitudes toward outsiders that sort very ill with the usual conception of the Johannine "love ethic."

Before we go on, it would be well to clarify my statement that in John God's concern is for the disciples and not for the world. Stated thus baldly, this is obviously an exaggeration, for of course John 3:16

declares that it was God's love for the world that caused the sending of the only Son. Marinus de Jonge points out in fact that in John 1–12 references to the world are mostly positive, while in John 13–20 and in 1 John they are mostly negative. The positive references relate largely to God's intention to save the world in the mission of the Son, the negative ones to the situation of the community in the world after Jesus' departure.[33] Thus, when considered in relation to God's will, the world can be redeemed and is the object of God's love; but considered concretely, in its response to God's Son and to those who have become God's children through him, the world seems irredeemably hostile. John does nothing to explain or to mitigate this paradox, and the paradox itself may suggest the condition of a group whose increasing sectarianism was in conflict precisely with the love ethic it had inherited.[34]

Could Johannine Christianity include a love of enemies? That is a question we cannot answer. The gospel and the epistles simply do not speak of such a love, and we can hardly go behind them to ask what their author (or authors) *might* have spoken of. The First Epistle of John, indeed, says that God loved us when we did not love God (1 John 4:10), but it does not go on to say that we should love those who do not love us. "Let us love one another," it says, but, "Do not love the world" (1 John 4:7; 2:15). The gospel, if its attitude toward the world is at least more paradoxical than that of the epistles, still does not draw any more positive ethical conclusions. The Johannine attitude toward outsiders (let alone enemies), while not explicitly hateful, is nevertheless much more one of mistrust and even bitterness than love.

This attitude may be clearly seen, for example, in John 8:31–47. In this passage Jesus argues with "Jews who have believed in him" but who do not think they need *his* word to make them free. He claims that they seek to kill him, and denounces them bitterly as children, neither of Abraham nor of God, but of the devil. Ultimately they pick up stones to throw at him. The precise group of outsiders in view here is rather uncertain: they may be non-Christian Jews, but more likely they are Christian Jews (related to the Nicodemus group) who reject the Johannine claim of divinity for Jesus, and perhaps even collaborate in violent measures taken against the Johannine group.[35]

One can appreciate the situation of oppression that lies behind this text. The threat to Jesus' life very likely stands for a threat to the Johannine Christians' lives. But the historical Jesus never called any person the devil's child and never denied that any Israelite was a child of Abraham—or of God. The dehumanization of the enemy, characterizing the enemy as in essence something other than oneself, as inherently inferior or demonic, is a danger implicit in the distinction between the group and the world that runs throughout John's gospel, and we see here that it is a danger John does not wholly avoid. It is just this dehumanization that allows systematic and systemic violence against the enemy to be carried out, including at least some forms of revolutionary violence. Once again, John does not explicitly contemplate such violence. Yet a groundwork for violence is laid such that, given the opportunity, the oppressed may simply exchange places with their oppressors and continue the pattern of oppression in reverse against their ancient enemies. This is not mere pacifist theorizing. It is what actually happened in the fourth and fifth centuries, when Christianity allied itself with the power of the world and began a long and evil history of persecution against the Jews—basing itself in part on just such dehumanizing Johannine texts as this one. Johannine sectarianism and its ultimate result, then, must be taken into consideration when relating this gospel and its love ethic to the themes of liberation.

The love ethic of John does have positive meaning for liberation, however, and this meaning has been forcefully expounded by Miranda in his book *Being and the Messiah*. Since this work is perhaps not as well known as it deserves to be, I will summarize a portion of his discussion here before going on to consider his claims.

Miranda points to the connection that John makes between knowing and loving Jesus on the one hand and keeping his word or commandment on the other. This commandment is the commandment of love for one another; it is those who keep it who love Jesus, and it is to them that he makes himself known. But for John it is in Jesus, and only in him, that God also is known. Thus according to Miranda, John declares that God is known only in the keeping of the commandment to love one's neighbor. This is the "word that was God," for the biblical God is known only as the absolute imperative of love to others. Jesus revealed God because his good works were the works of God.[36]

But this revelation of God aroused the world's hostility, Miranda says, precisely because it consisted of love to others and the commandment to love others. Crucial here is the concept of "good works." Miranda holds on the basis of New Testament and Jewish evidence that "good works" is not a general expression but a precise technical term referring to helping those who are in need.[37] It is Jesus' "good works" in this sense that reveal God, and it is these good works that cause the world to hate Jesus. Because these are the messianic good works, the signal of the eschaton, they are an attack on the oppressive world as it is, and the world responds with violence.[38]

The world rejects Jesus because of his "good works." By the same token, according to John 3:19–20, it also rejects him because its own works are evil, so that conversely it is those who are disposed to do the "good works" of love and justice who accept him and so become children of God (John 1:12–13).[39] Hence it is not surprising that the Johannine Christians are known as such by their love for one another and are said to do the "works" of Jesus and greater works still.[40] It is adherence to the commandment of love that sets the community apart from the world, and as with Jesus, so also for them, the love of neighbor arouses the world's hatred. It does so, Miranda says, because their "good works" proclaim the eschatological transformation of the world and its social systems on the basis of love and justice.[41]

I cannot begin here to lay out the exegetical basis for Miranda's conclusions. Certainly it is not without flaws. Whether the Jewish conception of "good works" can be transferred wholesale into the Fourth Gospel, for instance, will be doubted by many. It is also definitely a misinterpretation, as I have said, to equate Johannine love for one another with Jesus' love for the neighbor. Moreover, in discussing the relation of the eucharistic passage in John 6 to the Farewell Discourses, we have seen that the "word" of Jesus most likely refers to the Johannine christological confession rather than directly to the commandment of love. We saw also, however, that those who keep this word must of necessity be those who love one another in the face of the world's hatred and hostility. Conversely, for this very reason only those who keep the commandment of love truly abide in the christological "word." For how can they remain faithful to it under persecution other than by remaining faithful to the oppressed community of those who believe in it? The revelation of God in Jesus, that is, in the Johannine confession of him, inevitably includes the love of one another. Indeed, it may well be doubted whether the two are really separable, any more than birth from water and birth from spirit.

Thus in spite of difficulties there are points at which Miranda's radicalism interprets this most radical of the gospels with daunting accuracy. That, as Miranda claims, for John the definitive eschatological act of God has already entered the world in Jesus is absolutely certain on the basis of all modern study of the Fourth Gospel. Only an individualist and "spiritualizing" tradition makes it seem inconceivable to us a priori that John could have meant this in a social sense. To be sure, John calls what is given by this act "life," and life is an individual possession and may, in John, be entirely "spiritual." But what conclusion should we draw from the fact that the signal manifestation of the eschatological reality in John is not an individual trait (e.g., "knowledge") but a social one, namely, love? I cannot see that Miranda errs in claiming that, for John, keeping the word of Jesus is intimately related to the knowledge of God and therefore to eternal life. Correct knowledge and acknowledgment of Jesus, so indispensable for John, are inseparable from the keeping of both the Johannine christological confession and the love commandment. Eternal life is thus not a private acquisition that carries with it as an incidental consequence an attitude of charity toward one's fellow believers. Rather, eternal life itself is socially constituted, in that it comes only to those who acknowledge Jesus by keeping his word, which includes the word of love. Eternal life presupposes not only the believer and Jesus who is believed but also the social context within which alone this word can be kept. Likewise the eschatological act of God that has taken place encounters the world not only in individual acts of decision but as a historical, social fact, the community where love is practiced.

But is this love concrete? Is it correct to speak of a community where love is practiced rather than one where love is talked about? Clearly we have little access to actual relationships within the Johannine community. Yet in John 15:12–13 the highest potentiality of the disciples' love is said, based on Jesus' love for them, to be the laying down of one's life for one's friends. In the community's threatened situation (cf. 16:2), this need not have been merely rhetorical, as we have emphasized before. The First Epistle of John interprets just this understanding of love to mean that within the brotherhood those who have a living must not shut their hearts against those in need (1 John 3:16–17). This is surely not a purely hypothetical problem, nor is there reason to think that the epistle, though written in a different situation, misrepresents the intention of the original Johannine tradition. Miranda is correct, then, in drawing from this text the conclusion that Johannine love is not an abstract or a theoretical virtue but was to be realized concretely in the situation of the oppressed.[42]

Miranda is also clearly correct to relate the love within the community to the world's hatred of it. The sequence of love commandment and hatred by the world in John 15, along with Miranda's other evidence, seems adequate textual proof of this.[43] We have already suggested that this relation arose from the need for communal solidarity against persecution by the synagogue authorities. Miranda, however, sees the causation as running in the opposite direction, the world's hostility being provoked by the community's love; and very likely there is once again a dialectic at work. It may be that an already existing solidarity within the Johannine community, extending across ethnic, gender, and perhaps class boundaries, and attributed by the group to its adherence to Jesus, served as a further and especial irritant to the authorities. Certainly from the Johannine viewpoint "the world" saw in the community the continuation of Jesus' testimony that its own works were evil (John 3:19–20; 7:7; 15:18–27). Once again, we must allow Miranda to prod us away from conceiving of these "evil works" in only the vaguest sort of way.[44] Something concrete may equally well be meant. Since the only ethical contrast spoken of in John is love and hate, it seems permissible to identify the world's "evil works," as the Johannine community saw them, with acts of hate, that is, not unreasonably, with acts of violence and oppression, directed against the community but felt to characterize the conduct of "the world" in general. The community of love stands as witness against the hatred in the world, and so draws that hatred down upon itself.

What are the results of our reflections on liberation and John's ethic of love? First, the existence of the community of love itself has emerged as a significant factor in understanding John. For the Fourth Gospel, the life that is God's gift belongs to those who take their place in this community, where love and action for the sake of others are to replace the world's oppression and self-interest. Within the community, relationships are established not on the basis of rank or class but on the basis of the love that obtains among those who are, all alike, children of God through their faith in God's Son. The existence of their community in mutual love, their laying down of life for one another, is itself the sign of their adherence to the one whom God has sent. Thus the absence of oppression among them is what indicates that *here* God's eschatological act has been recognized and affirmed. Even if such love is directed only inward toward one another and not outward toward the neighbor in the world, what are its implications for a church that includes both rich and poor, both powerful and powerless? In what is it known that God is acknowledged as God here, that a decision of faith has been made here? How will everyone know who "those who believe in his name" are?

And what will happen when they find this out? In John, those who are known as disciples of Jesus (e.g., the blind man) suffer an unwelcome fate. Invariably it is those who show the world the possibility, and therefore the necessity, of living in love, living for others, without violence and without oppression, whom the world hates most passionately and exterminates most vigorously. This is even more true when they attempt to form countercultural movements or societies, as with the martyrs of the second and third centuries and the Anabaptists, with Martin Luther King and Clarence Jordan—and with the Johannine community. John is aware of this, that the world will not be converted by love or to love as long as the world has anything to say about it. But John also proclaims the biblical faith that the world does not have the *last* say, which belongs to God. God has acted to save the world; since the world refuses its salvation, God's act becomes its overthrow and defeat (John 16:33). There is a genuinely subversive consciousness at work in John, however "spiritualized" it may seem to be, which sees the community of God's children perpetually endangering the world, and therefore being endangered by it, precisely because it is the community of love.

But John's subversive sectarianism has its unhealthy side too, insofar as its love is only for one another and not for the neighbor in Jesus' sense, much less for the enemy. If the community's love does not reach beyond its own borders, its witness may be rejected by the world for that very reason and the world hardened in its oppression. Intolerable as it may seem, if love is not extended to the oppressors, they may never know of any other possible way of existence, and even if it frightens them into violence, it is the only hope for their conversion. Worst of all, a merely sectarian love runs the risk of creating new oppressors that live by their own violence against the newly powerless. "Love one another" is a word that must be kept; but the word that liberates the world is "Love your neighbor as yourself."

Conclusions

What I have said here by no means exhausts the possibilities of relating John to the themes of liberation. I have not spoken of the Spirit, whom John calls "the Paraclete," the Advocate, who represents the presence of Jesus to the community, uniting them with him and so alienating them from the world, against which it bears witness even as it strengthens them. I have said nothing about the position of women, whose exercise of independent and unconventional roles in John raises significant questions about their status in the Johannine community.[45] The apparent egalitarianism of the Fourth Gospel and its lack of a hierarchy to mediate between Christ and Christians is also significant. Though there is much more that could be said, I must now simply pull together the themes of the foregoing study and survey the patterns that have emerged.

If nothing else, I hope it has been made plain that John is relevant to social and political issues, and in particular to the situation of the oppressed. As the symbolic story of Nicodemus shows, adherence to Jesus, and so to God's action in the world, is not something that can be privately given so as to avoid the world's hostility. Those who know the truth, whatever their standing, must openly side with those who attest it and suffer for its sake. Otherwise they will find themselves co-conspirators with the world, their halfway measures unable either to halt the world's oppression or to give them a share in that reorientation toward God which John calls a new birth. They will not even understand either their own complicity or the opportunity that is open to them.

That opportunity and the risk that it entails are given by the coming of God's Son into the world, a coming that undermines the structures of power and authority by which the world attempts to defend itself against him. Pilate can neither grasp nor undo the sovereignty of God that confronts him, and Barabbas cannot be the one to assert it. The "King of the Jews" is he who is not of this world, who creates the community of those who hear his voice and draws their allegiance away from the world, its authorities, and its violence, toward God.

The Johannine Jesus is thus one whose alienation from the world is continuous with that of his disenfranchised and oppressed disciples, a Jesus who concentrates in his person their entire universe of meaning and of hope. Through his solidarity with them, he validates their worth against the contempt of their oppressors, enabling them to persevere and assuring them in the face of all the world's evidence to the contrary that they belong to God and their way leads to God.

This solidarity which the community has with Jesus against the world is enacted in the members' love for one another, the keeping of his commandment. We have seen the danger involved in such a love, directed so strongly inward toward the group's own members in the context of a dualistic sectarianism. Yet even so, it remains true that it is love, and so the reordering of relationships based on love, that signifies the community's adherence to the eschatological act of God and so constitutes it both the locus of God's eternal life here and now and a witness for God against the hatred that is in the world. It is this community, in its oppressed condition, its love, and its exclusive allegiance to God in God's Son, that the church is—or is not.

I must register some cautions about these results at this point. As I have said before, the situation of oppression lying behind the Fourth Gospel is not of the same origin or character as all oppressions in the world today, so that fruitful comparisons cannot be drawn in every case. Many will find John's vivid and intransigent dualism uncongenial to the task of liberation or of theology in general. I must also note candidly that there is little or no direct evidence in John of what we would regard as a concrete political strategy, nor have I made any attempt to outline a Johannine praxis for liberation today. Nevertheless, I maintain that it is not true that the Fourth Gospel is "apolitical," that it simply withdraws from social and political questions. John is not "spiritual" in that sense.

If this study has accomplished anything, it has begun a work whose full implications remain to be unfolded. John, too, must be allowed to bear fruit for the liberation of people from injustice, and I hope that the lines laid down here may prove suggestive, within their limitations, for the theologians of liberation and their work. That there is something radical about the gospel of John is not difficult to see. It was a mistake to think that this radicalism could be content with things as they are, could offer only a "spiritual" or inward message that would allow the orders of the world to go about their business unopposed. John presents us with a Jesus who comes into the world to testify to the truth. This truth is the reality of God, the reality that God enters the world of God's own making to redeem it. The world's works, however, are evil, and these evil works keep it from remaining in the word of Jesus. Yet if it remained in his word, it would know the truth; and John does not say that knowing the truth will make us wise, or happy, or even good. Rather, he says, "You shall know the truth, and the truth shall make you free."

NOTES

1. I regret that I was unable to examine the doctoral dissertation of Hugo C. Zorilla on John 7–10, *La fiesta de liberación de los oprimidos* (Pontifical University of Salamanca; published by Editorial SEBILA, San José, Costa Rica). Zorilla's conclusions are summarized in "The Feast of Liberation of the Oppressed: A Rereading of John 7:1—10:21," *Mission Focus* 13 (1985) 21–24.

2. Frederick Herzog, *Liberation Theology: Liberation in the Light of the Fourth Gospel,* 22.

3. José Porfirio Miranda, *Being and the Messiah: The Message of St. John,* 27–70.

4. Ibid., 56–68, 81–90, 156–202.

5. Ibid., 96–100.

6. Ibid., 135–153.

7. On the latter, cf. ibid., 127–129.

8. Cf. Meeks, "Man from Heaven," 69.

9. Cf. Wengst, *Gemeinde,* 59.

10. Herzog, *Liberation Theology,* 61–67.

11. Cf. Bultmann, *Gospel of John,* 654–655.

12. Cf. Miranda, *Being and the Messiah,* 95–102. I will consider the meaning of good and evil works more closely when discussing John's love ethic below.

13. Miranda, ibid., 137–148.

14. See, as only a few examples, James H. Cone, *Black Theology and Black Power,* 34–38; Alfredo Fierro, *The Militant Gospel,* 152–171; and Leonardo Boff, "Christ's Liberation via Oppression: An Attempt at Theological Construction from the Standpoint of Latin America," in *Frontiers of Theology in Latin America* (ed. Rosino Gibellini), 100–132.

15. Meeks, "Man from Heaven," 68.

16. Ibid., 57, 60–67.

17. Ibid., 69–70.

18. Ibid., 71.

19. On the relation of John's Christology to the community's experience, especially its experience of suffering, see also Wengst, *Gemeinde,* 101–117.

20. Cf. Brown, *Gospel According to John,* 1:1xxv.

21. Marinus de Jonge, "The Son of God and the Children of God," in de Jonge, *Jesus,* 151–153.

22. Benjamin E. Mays, *The Negro's God, as Reflected in His Literature,* 14–15, 23–26, 59, and passim.

23. James H. Cone, *God of the Oppressed,* 13–14; the quotation is from p. 13.

24. Ibid., 32–33; cf. 114, 140–141.

25. Ibid., 124–125.

26. Cf. "Black Theology in 1976," a statement by the Theological Commission of the National Conference of Black Churchmen, in *Black Theology: A Documentary History, 1966–1979* (ed. Gayraud S. Wilmore and James H. Cone), 342–343.

27. This is reflected in J. Louis Martyn's conception of a "two-level drama" in John. Cf. Martyn, *History and Theology,* 37–41, 60–62.

28. Cone, *God of the Oppressed,* 32.

29. Käsemann, *Testament,* e.g., pp. 26, 65–66, 77.

30. Brown, *Community,* 109–144; and idem, *The Epistles of John,* 69–86. Cf. Miranda, *Being and the Messiah,* 156–170.

31. This limitation of Johannine love was rightly stressed by Käsemann, *Testament,* 59–60. Käsemann, however, then mistakenly attempted to isolate John 3:16 as uncharacteristic of the Fourth Evangelist on this basis. Cf. the discussion below.

32. Cf. Fernando Segovia, "The Love and Hatred of Jesus and Johannine Sectarianism," *CBQ* 43 (1981) 258–272.

33. De Jonge, "Son of God," in de Jonge, *Jesus,* 154–157.

34. See also the discussion of this paradox in relation to the Johannine mission in chapter 7 below.

35. Cf. Brown, *Community,* 76–78; Martyn, "Glimpses," 109–115; and Miranda, *Being and the Messiah,* 162–163.

36. Miranda, *Being and the Messiah,* 112–125, and esp. pp. 126–155.

37. Ibid., 97–98.

38. Ibid., 102–109.

39. Ibid., 93–96.

40. Ibid., 206, 209–210.

41. Ibid., 108–109, 127–129, 212–214.

42. Ibid., 94–95.

43. Ibid., 127–129.

44. Rudolf Bultmann was correct that the world's evil works and its sin are its rejection of Jesus and therefore of God (*Gospel of John,* 293–294, 551); but inseparable from this is the rejection of the word of love.

45. See Käsemann, *Testament,* 29, 31; and especially Sandra M. Schneiders, "Women in the Fourth Gospel and the Role of Women in the Contemporary Church," *BTB* 12 (1982) 35–45; and Brown, *Community,* 183–198.

7
Sect, World, and Mission: Johannine Christianity Today

Those who hope for Johannine theology to speak to contemporary Christianity and to the contemporary world are faced with a serious problem, arising from our new awareness of John's destination in the concrete social and theological situation of a specific community at a specific time. This difficulty has been admirably summarized by Georg Richter.

> Much that people have labelled, and still label today, as mystical vision in the Fourth Gospel, and as the result of the working of the Paraclete, has entirely unmystical causes: it is simply the dialogue with the harsh reality of a particular situation—namely the debate with the Jewish questioning of the divinity of Jesus—that underlies the statements and formulations of the gospel of John and gives them their peculiar character. . . . As soon as one detaches this Johannine "theology" from its concrete contemporary situation and generalizes it, one will inevitably misunderstand and overburden it. The result is then no longer "Johannine" theology, but at best theological speculation on statements of John's gospel.[1]

This is the issue I want to treat in this final chapter: How can the gospel of John, now clearly seen to be so intimately involved in the particular conflicts of a particular time and place, be of significance for us in our time and place? When it was still possible to take for granted the universality of John as the "spiritual gospel," this was not a problem. Nor was it a problem for the largely ahistorical existentialist interpretation proposed by Rudolf Bultmann. Now, however, that John's anchorage in historical circumstances and contingencies has once again been recovered and brought to the fore, we are confronted with no small dilemma.

Johannine Christianity bears many of the marks of a sect, of a movement that finds light and truth within its own community and falsehood and darkness outside. Precisely this sectarianism sums up the things that seem to render John so intractable for theological interpretation. It emphasizes the particularity, and indeed the idiosyncrasy, of this gospel and the community behind it. It points to both the sharp conflicts in which the community was involved and the symbolic universe that apparently distinguished it from much of the rest of early Christianity. Yet it is just this sectarian character of Johannine Christianity on which I intend to focus in exploring the contemporary significance of the Fourth Gospel. For I want us to bear in mind that the church is never more true to itself than when it remembers its origin as a sect, as a minority opinion, countercultural and antiestablishment. Questioning the rightness of things as they are has again and again been the spark of the church's renewal and the hallmark of its faithfulness to the gospel.

Thus I intend in this chapter to make the beginnings of a theological evaluation of Johannine sectarianism as we have been exploring it. I should say at the outset that I am aware that the use of the term "sect" carries with it a number of overtones that cannot always be controlled by the user. I do not mean to implicate early Christianity in general or Johannine Christianity in particular in the kind of dead-end irrationality and fractiousness that so often come to mind when people speak of "sectarianism." What I intend to imply by referring to Johannine Christianity as a "sect" will be seen clearly below and was summarized in the preceding paragraph: a minority counterculture consciously opposed to much of the status quo in its environment. It is not necessary to think of John's community, or of other early Christians, as occupying the *lunatic* fringe; but one can hardly deny that Christianity, in its beginnings, was a fringe group, whatever seeds of its later dominance, for good or for ill, it may already have carried within it. What I propose to do here is to evaluate this characteristic as it applies to the Fourth Gospel. Is John's sectarianism a wholly and inevitably negative thing? Or are there points about it that may be of positive value for contemporary Christianity? It is not likely that I shall be able to answer this question in all possible detail and depth. It will be enough to draw a few conclusions in the hope that future interpretation of John and Johannine sectarianism may take them much farther.

It would not be unreasonable in the situation Richter describes to feel a sense of loss: something at once familiar and profound seems to have been taken away from us, and something odd, uncomfortable, and perhaps not at all profound set in its place. Let me repeat here what I said in chapter 1, that I do not claim that the classical, "spiritual" interpretation of the Fourth Gospel is no longer possible or appropriate, only that such an interpretation must now take full account of the nature and origin of this gospel. The "spiritual" and the "sociological" interpretations of John must now be brought into relation to one another. As we have seen, for John even being "born from above" is not simply an individual spiritual experience but a social one as well, the making of a dangerous public confession of faith in Jesus' messiahship and of adherence to his disciples. The Johannine dualism between spirit and flesh, the world above and the world below, is not a dualism between interior and exterior, personal and social. The realm of the spirit includes both interior and exterior, and so does the realm of the flesh. It is not that the world above is that of the individual and God, while the world below is that of society. Rather, there is a society that is "of this world" but also a society that is "from above," namely, the community of the Johannine Christians. To interpret John "spiritually" does not mean to interpret it ahistorically or asocially. It means to set forth John's claims about the meaning of encounter with God in Jesus Christ for all the dimensions of human existence, personal, social, and historical, for the individual believer and for the believing community.

And the mere recognition of the Fourth Gospel's sectarianism and particularity does not render it meaningless for other times and circumstances. For it remains true that the gospel of John presents a solution greater than the problems with which it was faced. Written in a situation of conflict and oppression, and with all the limitations imposed by adherence to one party in a hard-fought and many-sided struggle, the gospel of John refuses to restrict that struggle to its own terms of time, place, and society but connects it instead to the deepest issues of God's relation to the world and the human race, and of the human response to God and to one another.[2] At issue was the messiahship of Jesus. For John, this became an issue of reality itself, of "truth," as he calls it, and of faith, and of love. John goes far beyond midrash and prooftexting to argue from the Christians' own experience of God, and does so, moreover, in a dense and original symbolic language. If this language serves to make the text all but opaque to the newcomer or the outsider who does not know or admit its central secret, it also attracts and draws in by its very mysteriousness and its convoluted self-containment.[3] The language of John is a kind of enchanting barrier, an irresistible obstacle that advertises a treasure within and yet seems designed to make the treasure all but inaccessible. Understanding comes, not when the barrier has been surmounted and the obstacle defeated, but in the very process of trying to penetrate it. It is precisely in the midst of John's hall of mirrors that one looks and sees every surface reflect the face of Christ. Even the community's oppressed situation does not simply interpret itself but is, rather, interpreted in the light of the good and evil that are exposed when humanity confronts the God confronting it. In one sense, the struggle of the Johannine community becomes a paradigm for the great struggle that results when God's will to redeem the world engages the world's unwillingness to be redeemed. In another sense, it is not a paradigm but a metaphor for that larger struggle, that is, it implies the whole of it in its own small compass. We see the Logos of God's redemption here in the flesh of a Jewish Christian community's struggle with the synagogue in the late first century. It is the Logos that has made the Fourth Gospel the object of the church's concentrated attention for all these centuries. Yet that fleshly struggle retains its own identity, and its own significance for understanding John and for understanding redemption and liberation.

Implications of Johannine Sectarianism

As we saw in chapter 1 above, the Johannine community may reasonably be regarded as a sectarian group with introversionist characteristics. Nevertheless, it had apparently not completely given up on the possibility of mission to the world. The group's sectarianism may be seen primarily in its relations with Judaism and in its attitude toward the outside world as a whole, though we have also noted in previous chapters ways in which it may have at least differed with other Christian groups. It is now time to consider some of the implications of this depiction.

The negative aspects of Johannine sectarianism are not difficult to see. In a sectarian setting, John's dualism could, as suggested in chapter 6, above, rather easily give rise to a xenophobia that would have little room for ordinary kindness, let alone self-giving love, toward outsiders. Separation from the world, which is regarded as the realm of darkness in contrast to the fellowship of light within the sect, all too readily degenerates into suspicion, fear, and even hatred of the world. In the situation of persecution in which the Johannine community found itself, this would be a particularly likely outcome, and indeed a response of suspicion and fear would not have been entirely unreasonable. Given such a passage as John 15:18–16:4a, we may be glad that the Fourth Evangelist does not in fact bid the "Sons of Light" to "hate all the Sons of Darkness," as the Qumran *Manual of Discipline* does (1QS 1:9–10).

Even so, however, there are other dangers. Certainly it would be possible for a Christianity inspired by John to come to regard itself as the sole possessor of truth, which, after all, the world does not know unless it remains in the word of Jesus, as the community does (John 8:32). Such a Christianity might find itself unable to hear any truth spoken by those outside its own circle and so cut itself off from further possibilities of knowing both God and other human beings. Equally dangerous is the sort of "dogmatic hardening" of which Ernst Käsemann speaks.[4] Having the truth, the community would have no obligation greater than to protect it, and this could most easily be done by codifying it in formulas that must then be immutable, and become objects of faith in themselves. There are features of the Fourth Gospel that work to protect against such dangers, as we shall see; but the dangers remain real for any Christianity that bases itself seriously on the gospel of John.

It is for such reasons that ecumenism in its various forms is one area of contemporary theology for which Johannine sectarianism seems particularly hazardous. Let me speak first about relations between Jews and Christians. As we saw in chapter 6, the denunciation of "the Jews" that pervades the Fourth Gospel, found at its most virulent in such a passage as 8:31–47, has all too often been used by Gentile Christians to justify their own self-righteous sense of superiority and, worse yet, their acts of persecution and discrimination against Jews. John's sectarian hostility toward outsiders thus has led and could easily lead again to injustice and violence. Even if such extreme consequences are avoided, John gives little encouragement to Christians and Jews seeking calm and open dialogue with one another. Therefore it is just here that the historical circumstances of this gospel's origin must be carefully considered before any theological conclusions, or even any theological proposals, are drawn from it. It is a fact that Johannine Christianity arose from the persecution of one group of Jews by another because of their confession of Jesus. No one living today owes anyone else an apology because of that. For history has long since passed that situation by; and for this very reason we must frankly declare that the gospel of John is of no use in attempting to establish, or reestablish, Christian-Jewish relationships today.[5] There are no Christians being persecuted as such by the synagogue in our world; on the other hand, the persecution of Jews by Christians has continued and does continue to this day. Indeed, the condemnation of John 16:2 falls, as it has fallen for centuries, on Christian rather than on Jewish heads. Because the gospel of John is so intimately tied to a state of relations between Jews and Christians that no longer exists, and that ceased to exist shortly after the gospel was written, it must simply be ruled out of order in seeking a foundation for contemporary Christian-Jewish relations. Only the wrong that has been done in John's name—and done twice wrongly, since John was written for the use of an oppressed community and not for that of oppressors—must be acknowledged and repented before the book can be laid aside in this context.

What about relationships among Christian groups? Again John's sharply sectarian sense of isolation and his dogmatic insistence on right confession of Jesus poses problems. Käsemann, who was perhaps the first in recent times to point out the dogmatic nature of Johannine Christology,[6] did not really pursue the question from this angle. Raymond Brown, in depicting the history of the Johannine community, suggested that christological dogma did in fact lead it first to dissension with other Christian groups and then to schismatic dissolution within itself.[7] Once again, we will see shortly some of the safeguards that John contains against such drawing of dogmatic boundaries against other Christians. Nevertheless, it must be acknowledged that John's introverted sectarianism yields a poor model for those seeking rapprochement among the various forms of contemporary Christianity. It is all too much concerned with safeguarding the existence of an oppressed community and its boundaries against the world to be of great use in building bridges across boundaries.

In spite of problems such as these, I think it worth the effort to seek at least some positive values in John's sectarianism, for I believe that only in this way can we truly and honestly affirm the worth of the Fourth Gospel. In the first place, a truly Johannine Christianity would be one that was plainly and even assertively based on a forthright confession of Jesus Christ. It was such a confession that brought the Johannine group into conflict with the synagogue authorities, and the confession was further shaped and strengthened by that conflict. Both in the eyes of the group and, apparently, in the eyes of outsiders their most distinctive and irreducible feature was their confession of Jesus as Messiah and Son of God, and indeed as one who transcended even such categories as "messiah" and "king," who could not be acknowledged merely as an eschatological prophet like John the Baptist or as one teacher among many in the style of the Pharisees. It was their insistence on this confession, and on making it in a public and dangerously recognizable way, that may have separated them to some extent even from other Christians.[8] Thus the Johannine community's confession was indissolubly linked to their sectarianism. It may be that, for this very reason among others, the Johannine christological confession will be seen by many as not an especially positive thing. Let me go on, therefore, to explore a few of its particular features.

Johannine Christology must be understood as the foundational vision of John's Christianity, the reality—the "truth"—in which the community's sense of God, of themselves, and of others was grounded. Yet this grounding reality is expressed in a very peculiar way. In spite of Käsemann, John's statement of his Christology is not particularly "dogmatic." To be sure, the creation of confessing faith in Jesus as Messiah and Son of God is the very goal of the book (John 20:31). But this confession is not presented as a "fact," as a dogmatic formulation to be accepted as if it were a scientific axiom. We must recall what was said above about the character of Johannine language. The use of symbolism, irony, and double entendre, and the "mysterious" quality of Johannine style, so difficult to analyze and yet so undeniably present, always prevents the "dogmatic" Christology of the Fourth Gospel from becoming a mere creed to be subscribed to. The *meaning* of Jesus' messiahship and Sonship is never exhausted by any particular expression of it, whether declarative or poetic; and it is the meaning that John wants his readers to appropriate for themselves, never the words alone. It is for this reason too that the Fourth Gospel repeatedly presents diametrically opposed statements about Jesus: the Logos was with God, and yet the Logos was God (1:1); Jesus is one with the Father, and yet the Father is greater than he (10:30; 14:28); he is both the Good Shepherd and the Door through which sheep and shepherd enter (10:7, 11). John does not ask us to resolve these contradictions or to construct a rational synthesis in which both statements might be equally true. His intent is precisely that we move back and forth between the opposing poles, accepting not only each of the contradictory statements but the fact of their contradiction as well. It is only *in this process itself* that we can begin to perceive the truth, for the truth does not lie at either end of any of the diametrical oppositions, nor in the middle between them, nor in some combination of them. Rather, the truth is what each of these statements reflects and yet no such statement can truly express. The words of Jesus are this truth, which is also the word he heard from God (8:40, 45; 17:17); yet above all he himself *is* this truth (14:6). No dogmatic formulation can contain this truth, nor can its content be definitively expressed for all time even within the Johannine community, even by the Johannine gospel itself. That is the meaning of the promise that the Spirit of Truth will lead the community into all truth (16:13).

This lessens, though it does not eliminate, the difficulty of John's sectarian claim to exclusive possession of the truth. For as Käsemann affirms, John's christological "dogma" is always subject to kerygmatic development in new situations, and, like the Johannine church itself and the Johannine sacraments, must always point not to itself but beyond itself to Jesus.[9] A really Johannine Christianity will never be content to point to its own beliefs, statements, liturgies, and rituals as if assent to these were what God required. The sectarian Johannine Christology itself forbids it. The Christology that defined the Johannine sect demanded adherence to a community, a fact whose significance we shall explore later in the chapter. But its most fundamental demand was for an encounter, not with a church or a dogma, a religion or a morality, but with God.[10]

There is also this: it was precisely this radical Christology which enabled the community of the Fourth Gospel to undertake their radical commitment to God in the face of dire risk. This was not the petty risk of social discomfort that prevents most of us from making even the slightest move toward nonconformity. Nor was it the more or less theoretical "risk" involved in making an existential "decision" in the privacy of one's soul. People staked all that they had and all that they were or appeared to be on their confession of Jesus as Messiah and Son of God. The social and religious context that gave their lives shape and meaning, even their own families (as in the case of the blind man), even life itself, could be lost here. If Christianity is to undertake so demanding a commitment in any area today, it must have an equally demanding foundation. The Christ of John did not come to judge the world, nor yet to change it from within, but to save it. That meant to recall it from its self-absorption to its stance as creature before its Creator, yielding an obedience to God that could undo the structures that maintained it apart from God in the darkness of its hatred. If a world of violence, hard dealing, and pain is to be challenged and undone today, can it be on any lesser basis than the Logos of God that would see the world made whole? And that entered the world, at its own risk, to make it so?

For, above all, the meaning of John's sectarianism is that *because it was sectarian* it challenged the world on the basis of the love of God and the word of God. No religion that sees itself as the backbone of a society, as the glue that holds a society together, can easily lay down a challenge to that society's wrongs. A cultural religion is all too readily told to mind its own business, because it *has* a business, a well-known role in maintaining society's fabric unmolested. It is the sect, which has no business in the world, that is able to present a fundamental challenge to the world's oppressive orders. Precisely because it sees itself alienated from the world, its commitment to the world's orders is attenuated, if not abolished altogether. Thus it is able to take a stand over against the world and to criticize that which the world holds most dear. It is free to question unquestionable assumptions and to challenge unchallengeable conclusions. It is free to expose the deceptions (including the self-deceptions) by which the world holds itself upright, the blindness that the world regards as sight. The sect, like the child in the fairy tale who has no position in society to defend, is able to state what it sees, that the emperor is naked after all.

In the case of the Johannine community, its christological commitment left it free to opt out of the world's structures and to stand over against them. This was not only because the world rejected its Christology but because the Johannine Jesus gave the group a place to stand when the world denied it one. Because the community of the Fourth Gospel saw in Jesus the transcendent fulfillment of all that it was losing in the synagogue, and indeed the locus of divine creation, redemption, and life, it was able to lose its place in the world without losing its hope and its confidence—not without feeling distress and fear; otherwise such words as John 14:27; 16:33 would not have had to be written. Yet a Johannine Christianity would be able, for the sake of its commitment to God, to let loose its commitment to the world and to be without a place in it. A Johannine Christianity would be set free to criticize the world's injustice and violence in the name of the world's Creator who calls the creature to return. It is characteristic of Johannine sectarianism that it calls for a choice, and not merely a private one to be made in the comfort of one's own home. The choice is between God and the world, the world which reacts with violence and oppression against God and God's messenger; and it is a public choice, to be made in the discomfort of social exposure. It is precisely Johannine Christianity's nature as a sect that enables it to present that choice with radical clarity as a radical demand.

It is of course far too late in the day for Christianity as a whole to become sectarian once again. Yet it may be that in the Christian movements of the Third World, for instance, the Johannine sense of being outside the framework of a given society can come to be felt again. The same thing could also happen in some Western churches, those belonging to the smaller, free-church traditions, though for many of them a deliberate act might be necessary to recover the tradition of sectarianism. And even mainstream Christianity ought perhaps to greet the secularization of Western society with joy and hope rather than dismay. For the meaning of "secularization" is precisely that the world is to be known openly as the world again, and not pretend to be the church. Christianity, then, can once again be free to let itself be known as Christianity, *over against* the world of secular society and critical of its oppressive and ungodly structures. For some time now, in fact, this has already been taking place. Even some of the far-right fundamentalist groups in the United States must be granted the correct insight that Christianity has the need and the duty to speak a critical word of God to secular society. Their mistake lies partly in their wanting to take over secular society and "Christianize" it again and partly in their idolatrous identification of the United States—or indeed of white American males—with the chosen people of God. But if such groups have distorted and even betrayed the mission of Christianity, then it would be worth our while to inquire what John says that mission is.

The Johannine Mission

The image of the Johannine community as an introversionist sect would not seem to encourage the idea of a Johannine mission. Such groups have generally turned in upon themselves to the extent that they have given up on the world and lost all sense of mission to it.[11] But I have already suggested that Johannine Christianity is not a pure example of introversionism, and I want here to substantiate some aspects of that claim.

A recent study by Takashi Onuki is helpful in this regard. Onuki points out that the task of forgiving or retaining sins is given to the community by the risen Jesus in the context of their being sent as he was sent, and is oriented, not to community members only, but to "anyone" (John 20:21–23). Thus the community's mission is, like that of Jesus, to "take away the sin of the world," to draw people from darkness into light (1:29; 12:46). Like Jesus, the community is sent into the world with the revelation of God, and, like him, it meets with rejection.[12] The function of the Fourth Gospel, then, is to enable the community to step back from its situation of rejection, reflect upon it in the light of the fate of Jesus, and to be *sent out again with its faith renewed.* The Fourth Evangelist's dualism thus works not only to distance the community from the world but also to affirm both the community's identity and the possibility of conversion and salvation for people in the world.[13]

Onuki's interpretation of 20:21–23 is persuasive,[14] and his understanding of the function of the gospel is well worth considering. Clearly the Fourth Gospel throughout presents the community's position and work as those of Jesus himself, and not only 20:21 but at least 4:31–38 and 17:18 as well make it plain that this work is the mission to the world.[15] But equally clearly the Fourth Gospel itself is not a mission document.[16] As a whole it can hardly have been written with the purpose of bringing Jews, Samaritans, or anyone else to faith.[17] Precisely its sectarian sharpness and the "in-group" nature of its language tell against this.[18] But it could very readily serve (among other purposes) to sustain the Johannine community in its mission, as Onuki proposes. In its rereading of the gospel, the community would be reminded yet again of the purpose of Jesus' coming—that it was out of God's love for the world, not for the world's condemnation but for its salvation. Despite Käsemann's effort to do so, John 3:16–17 cannot be dismissed as uncharacteristic of the Fourth Gospel,[19] in the light not only of its immediate context but of John 1:29; 6:33; 10:10; 12:46–47. The community would also read of Jesus' testimony to the world and of its result, climaxing in his ultimate rejection on the cross; and it would find that its own fate was linked to that of Jesus by 12:23–26 and 15:18–20 if by nothing else. But 12:23 itself identifies the hour of Jesus' death as the hour of his glorification, and if this means that the Passion of Jesus is really his glorious return to the Father,[20] it also serves to interpret the suffering of the persecuted community. The suffering of the members, like his suffering, does not invalidate but rather validates their fidelity to God and God's love for them. Thus not only, with Onuki, would the Farewell Discourses serve to reaffirm the community's identity in its mission, but the Johannine Passion narrative and Passion conception would do so as well. And in the end the reading community would come again to its sending, empowered by the Spirit, to take away the sin of the world in 20:21–23.

Thus it appears that there was a mission for the Johannine community and that it had not become so introverted as to have turned its back definitively on the world. Our next question may be about the object of that mission. Onuki speaks exclusively of "the Jews" in this context, and as long as we think of "the world" in its narrowest sense in John this is correct. The Jewish synagogue community and its authorities may still have formed an important object of the Johannine mission, despite all the difficulties that had been encountered. We need not stop there, however. The dialogue with Nicodemus in John 3 could indicate that hope was still held out that the secret Christian Jews whom he represents would come to a full and open confession of Jesus as Messiah and Son of God,[21] just as the passage on John the Baptist that follows it implies an appeal to his disciples. Given the fact that immediately after these two somewhat difficult prospects for conversion we are told the story of Jesus' far more successful dialogue with the Samaritan woman, many scholars would agree that the Johannine community included Samaritans among its numbers,[22] and most likely we should therefore infer at least some ongoing Samaritan mission as well. Finally, the Greeks who wish to see Jesus in John 12:20–22 are widely and correctly interpreted as indicating a Johannine mission to Gentiles (cf. 7:35).[23] Thus, though the synagogue dispute is the paradigm case, "the world" in John as an object of God's love and the community's mission is by no means restricted to Pharisaic Judaism. No doubt in all these cases the community encountered both receptivity to its message and the resistance that typified for it the will of the world to remain in darkness.

This leads us to ask about the nature of the Johannine "world" in general as an object of Christianity's mission. To what does John refer when he uses this term? According to C. K. Barrett, the world in John is "the whole organized state of human society, secular and religious."[24] Albert Curry Winn, in a very useful recent study of the contemporary significance of Johannine mission, has defined the "world" as "human society as it is structured in opposition to Christ and to the followers of Christ."[25] Winn calls the world "a series of ordered, structured, interlocking systems" that are opposed to God because of their destruction of basic human values. "On a planet structured graciously by God, the dehumanizing structures that we have made, and in which we are trapped, roll on and on, grinding people to bits. . . . [These structures] seem to move us relentlessly toward an unthinkable holocaust." It is into *this* world that Christianity is sent.[26] José Porfirio Miranda, citing Barrett, formulates the matter even more radically: "The modern word 'civilization' provides a rough equivalent of John's pejorative use of 'the world': both refer to the sum total of the ways in which people function within and among themselves. John's pejorative 'world' . . . is neither an abstraction nor a universal but a supra-individual and eminently concrete reality that clearly refers to all of civilization and not only to any one civilization in particular." In John's affirmations of God's intention to save the world by the sending of Jesus Christ, " 'The world' . . . is humankind liberated from sinful civilization."[27]

It would seem, then, that Christianity must be prepared, on the basis of the Fourth Gospel, to hold a broad and yet highly specific understanding of "the world" to which it is sent. It is not the world of creation, of "nature" as such, of earth and sky, sexuality and labor, health and sickness, that is given us with our physical existence. Rather, it is the world as it has been structured by human will and rationality, but also and especially by human self-absorption and selfishness in opposition to God and to the good of other people.[28] In short, it is human society as such, as it is organized and maintained for the good of some but to the harm of others and to the detriment of the love of God. So, for John, evil does not lie in creation but in the human response to creation and to the Creator. Not that what is human is evil as such: the Logos is and remains the light of the human race, and Jesus appears as the fulfillment (even if also the transcendence) of many human hopes, as I will emphasize below. Thus what is meant by "the world" is not something essential (matter or human nature) but something willed and willful. Not everything human is evil; yet again and again humanity *prefers* the darkness.

But why does humanity do so? Why when the Logos came into the world did his own not receive him? John gives no etiology of evil, such as is found in gnosticism. He simply acknowledges as fact, as the actual experience of God's revelation, that it is met with human rejection.[29] Yet he does offer some explanation, for according to John 3:19 it was "because their works were evil" that people avoided the light. Note that John does not proceed to give a list of morally bad deeds (such as is found, for instance, in Mark 7:21–22 or 1 Cor. 6:9–10) that kept the world from being reconciled to God. He is concerned not with specifying the identity of the works but with their character as evil. We saw in chapter 6 that these "evil works" include acts of violence against the community, treated as characteristic of "the world's" conduct in general. The world's acts of hatred and its failure to love—that is, to do *acts* of love—are thus an integral part of its evil and its rejection of God and Christ. Indeed, according to John 7:7 it is precisely because Jesus testifies that the world's works are evil that it hates and rejects him.[30]

But the testimony of the Johannine community beyond question continues the testimony of Jesus himself (hence the "we" of John 3:11) and meets the same fate as his (15:20).[31] Thus the Johannine mission must include precisely this same testimony against the world's rejection of God in its rejection of love. A Johannine Christianity will have no message for the world if it does not have *this* message. It cannot call for repentance unless it calls for repentance from *this* evil, and it cannot declare sin forgiven or retained without speaking of *this* sin. The question of love and hate, of doing good or of doing violence—in our time, the questions of social justice and of peace—are not peripheral or subsidiary to the Johannine message about Jesus. They are, rather, of its essence, for the Johannine message is that Jesus came because of God's love and testified to the truth, that is, to his own bearing of the presence of God into the world. It was this testimony which showed the world's works to be evil; and the only good and evil of which John speaks are love and hatred. We must therefore conclude that the presence of God in the incarnate Logos is the presence of love challenging the world's hatred structured as violence and avarice, both personal and institutional. Jesus, coming into the world to bring it life, confronts its infatuation with death and with death-dealing systems. Johannine Christianity does no less, and can do no more, than to repeat, again and again, that confrontation. John calls this confrontation the world's *krisis,* its judgment, a judgment that it renders on itself by its reaction to the light (3:19). Johannine Christianity is called upon to bring about precisely this crisis, a critical point of decision for or against love in the decision for or against God.

But how is this done? How does Johannine Christianity confront the world with this decision? It does so, in part, by being what it is, the community of those who believe in Jesus the Messiah. For just as the world's hatred is part of its rejection of the message of Jesus, so the community of love is itself a part of the gospel. This is stated most plainly in John 13:34–35: the disciples of Jesus will be known by their keeping of his commandment of love. But it is implied in the very confession that both constitutes the community and is the message it proclaims: that Jesus is Messiah. The community that believes this believes that the eschatological action of God has already begun and that it itself lives in the messianic age, under God's eschatological blessing. I would reaffirm here my agreement with Miranda that for John the messianic event has broken into the world and that the Christian community is by its very nature the messianic community.[32] To confess Jesus as Messiah is to acknowledge that one lives *already* in the kingdom of God, for entrance into the kingdom is the goal of being "born from above," which comes from faith in Jesus and the public confession of it in baptism (John 1:12–13; 3:5). To live, through this confession, in the kingdom of God is to live under the kingship of Jesus, a kingship that is not of this world, and whose unworldly character is expressed precisely in his servants' refusal to take up arms in his defense (18:36). The kingship that is not established or defended by acts of violence is the kingship under which the messianic community lives, the community whose messianic identity is known in its love for one another. Thus its love and its refusal of violence are essential to its confession of the messiahship of Jesus and indispensable to its making that messiahship known. The love that characterizes the messianic community is integral to the gospel with which it confronts the world. This gospel is a call not simply to personal repentance and conversion but to join the messianic community. This is the message of Jesus to Nicodemus: *"You people* must be born from above."* The worldly *community* represented by Nicodemus must undergo a change of social location by openly acknowledging the messiahship of Jesus and in so doing become part of the messianic community. They are called on to abandon the world and its continuing self-centeredness and to be integrated into the community of love.

Other characteristics of the Johannine community are worth noting as well. It has sometimes been observed that, as remarked at the end of chapter 6 above, this community has no hierarchy. Käsemann, for instance, points out that the apostles are given no preferred status or ecclesiastical significance. John introduces various disciples unknown from lists of the Twelve, and the power of forgiving or retaining sins is given, with the gift of the Spirit, to the community as a whole.[33] The community thus appears as an egalitarian brotherhood, without distinctions of rank or dignity. And in fact it is more than a brotherhood, for, as Käsemann has emphasized and others have studied in detail, women play a noteworthy role in the Fourth Gospel.[34] Two women, the Samaritan and Mary Magdalene, bear the news of Jesus' messiahship and of his resurrection (John 4:28–29;

20:2, 17–18). In thus carrying out its mission within the gospel itself, they represent the Johannine community as a whole. The messianic community's egalitarianism is therefore another of the distinctive traits it bears before the world.

Studies of Johannine sectarianism, including my own, have tended to focus on its closedness and introversion. There are some aspects, however, in which it shows a marked and somewhat surprising openness. I have noted already the promise of 16:13 that the Spirit of Truth will lead the community into all truth. There is thus the prospect of coming into new understanding beyond what the group already has, a prospect whose serious acceptance by his opponents within the later Johannine community may have caused the author of 1 John to insist that his readers remain in that which they had heard from the beginning (1 John 2:24).[35] Moreover, I have also noted the diversity of groups that formed the object of the Johannine mission. None of these groups was without religious hopes and symbols of its own. George W. MacRae proposed in a highly suggestive article that the Fourth Evangelist deliberately incorporated a variety of symbols, traditions, and perspectives into his gospel in order to emphasize precisely the universality of Jesus. According to MacRae, for John no single conceptual mode, Jewish, Greek, or gnostic, was adequate to grasp the meaning of Jesus, who fulfilled them all without being fully captured by any one of them. The bewildering variety of Johannine "backgrounds" would thus have a positive value for interpretation.[36]

Whatever may be the validity of MacRae's proposal in detail, we may at least feel certain that the Johannine tradition was open to a wide variety of religious options corresponding to the variety of groups it addressed, and no doubt to a growing diversity of origin among its members. This counteracts to a considerable extent the sectarian danger of being closed off to other people and to the truth they may have to offer. Johannine Christology seems to have been extraordinarily flexible in the imagery and concepts it could incorporate in seeking to express the meaning of Jesus. The central confession of Jesus as Messiah, Son of God, giver of eschatological life, was impregnable; but the means of approaching or unfolding the content of this confession were extremely and no doubt deliberately diverse. As we observed above, there is in John no set of fixed dogmatic christological formulations. This means that the Johannine community saw and presented Jesus not as the denial but as the affirmation of many of the religious hopes that they encountered. With MacRae, they also saw these hopes transcended in Jesus, so that Jesus himself passed beyond the ultimate grasp of any one or any combination of them. Nevertheless, we see portrayed here a diversity and openness within the messianic community, grounded precisely in its christological confession. To be the community of Jesus the Son of God, this community could not close itself off against human expressions of longing for wholeness and salvation, because the community's encounter with Jesus had proven to be an encounter with that which would not be limited to any restricted set of such expressions. The community's openness and diversity were necessary features of its congruence with Jesus and the unbounded presence of God that it had found in him.

We may say, then, that the Johannine community confronted the world not merely with a doctrine or a creed but, as all sectarian groups do, with an alternative society, a counterculture, in which its message of the messiahship of Jesus was realized. It sought to draw people out of the world and into the messianic community, and it did this not only by its words but by *being* that community. It expressed in common life the love, equality, and openness appropriate to those who claimed that in Jesus the messianic bounty had come and the presence of God that transcends human self-centeredness had been made known. Johannine Christianity presents a challenge to the world's violence and injustice, its oppression, greed, and divisiveness. Among those who profess the kingship of Jesus, the world's idolatrous chauvinisms—of nation, race, gender, or otherwise—are dissolved. A Johannine Christian community will itself be the gospel, and it will confront the world with a reality that testifies against the world's own character but also offers it the alternative of eschatological life, begun *now* in communion with the one who is the resurrection and the life. Johannine Christianity confronts the world with the truth of Jesus and with its own existence in that truth as the community of messianic love. In thus standing against the world, it puts its own life in the world at risk, for it must always recall the words of Jesus before his Passion: "If anyone serves me, let that person follow me; and where I am, there will my servant be also" (John 12:26).

Johannine Christianity

In the end, one grows weary of explaining the Fourth Gospel. No explanation can be commensurate with the book itself, and the book itself does not claim to be commensurate with the reality to which it points. Let the reader open the text and begin. There is far more here than we can explain, account for, justify, or accommodate. Yet given our new understanding of it and the pressing new circumstances in which we read, there is good reason to consider this book again. It is not only that we may be able to understand John better than we or our predecessors have done. It is that John may help us to understand ourselves, our faith, and our time in a radically different manner than we have before. It did so for those who first read it long ago, and we too may have much to hope if we read faithfully and attentively.

Much of Christianity, in the United States at least but perhaps elsewhere as well, is severely divided today about what is the center, the essential heart, of its faith. For some it lies in doctrine, in the eternal truth about God and about Jesus Christ preserved in the scriptures and in Christian teaching. For some it is primarily ethical, the doing of good and the seeking of peace and justice for humankind. Many of the former, but not all of them and not only they, would see Christianity as essentially directed at the individual, at inner transformation and personal salvation. Others see its goal as the reformation of society, the healing of relationships and the creation of equitable social arrangements. There are many odd crossings and combinations among these views and among the Christians who hold them; but I hope this may serve as a reasonable summary of where we stand.

The gospel of John has not exactly been a battleground in these dissensions. By and large, it has been the property of those who hold a doctrinal and individualistic conception of what Christianity is about. It is not my intention to seize the Fourth Gospel and drag it over to the other, or another, side of this debate. Rather, I hope to have shown that the radical confession that created the Johannine community and its gospel may offer us the possibility of a contemporary Christianity whose dogmatic and ethical, individual and social dimensions are at last integrated into a single whole. The gospel of John makes an uncompromising claim about Jesus Christ. It demands of each individual a decision about that claim, and it insists on the validity and necessity of individual relationship with God through Jesus Christ. But the *specific* claim that it makes about Jesus, that as Son of God he confronts the human world with its own hatefulness, and the *specific* response that it calls for, a public response of integration into a community of love, overcome all narrowly dogmatic and individualist interpretations. The Johannine claim and the Johannine response challenge the world as it is and present it with a revolutionary alternative. Yet the ethical transformation toward love and the alternative vision of society that John offers are not something that can be attained simply through human effort or mass action. They are offered in the giving of God's Son through the love of God and in the community of individuals who have believed in him. It is this unitary vision, profoundly reflected on and expressed in a rich and difficult literary art, that the gospel of John makes available.

This, at any rate, cannot be explained any further. It is up to us to seize this vision in its unity—or rather, to be seized by it and to be ourselves made one. The renewal of self and society that John affords is one single renewal. The world's sin that Jesus takes away is *all* sin, not a selection from the realm of the personal or of the social. A single transformation that remakes thought and action, person and society, and makes them one: this is to be "born from above." This is Johannine Christianity.

NOTES

1. My translation is from Richter's German in "Die Gefangennahme Jesu nach dem Johannesevangelium (18, 1–12)," in *Studien zum Johannesevangelium,* by Georg Richter, 86.

2. We may take note here of similar observations made by two previous scholars. Marinus de Jonge ("Jewish Expectations about the 'Messiah' According to the Fourth Gospel," in de Jonge, *Jesus,* 100) remarks that John presents theological reflections on the issues arising from early Christian and Christian-Jewish debate in a way that goes beyond the particular situation itself. Takashi Onuki *(Gemeinde und Welt im Johannesevangelium,* 112, 140) observes that John does not remain on the level of his historically conditioned situation but operates on the more cosmic level of the dualism between "church" and "world."

3. On the function of Johannine language, see Herbert Leroy, *Rätsel und Missverständnis,* 46–47, 157, 167–170, 183–184; Meeks, "Man from Heaven," 68–71; Onuki, *Gemeinde,* 19–28; and Duke, *Irony,* 147–155.

4. Käsemann, *Testament,* 65.

5. Cf. Wengst, *Gemeinde,* 60–61.

6. Käsemann, *Testament,* 23–26, 49.

7. Brown, *Community,* 73–88, 109–123.

8. Not only from the crypto-Christians (cf. Brown, *Community,* 71–73; and Martyn, "Glimpses," 109–115) but even from other openly confessing Christians whose confession they did not regard as high enough (cf. Brown, *Community,* 73–88).

9. Käsemann, *Testament,* 40–45, 49–50.

10. Cf. Sandra M. Schneiders, "Reflections on Commitment in the Gospel According to John," *BTB* 8 (1978) 40–48.

11. Cf. Bryan R. Wilson, *Magic and the Millennium,* 23–24, 45.

12. Onuki, *Gemeinde,* 85–93.

13. Ibid., 102–115 (summarized on pp. 111–114). The same claim is made for the Farewell Discourses on pp. 95–101 and 131–141.

14. Lindars *(Gospel of John,* 613) had earlier taken a position that agrees in general with Onuki's.

15. In Käsemann's interpretation of the Fourth Gospel, too, "Christian life as such is mission" *(Testament,* 64).

16. Cf. Brown, *Gospel According to John,* 1:lxxiii–lxxiv, lxxviii; idem, *Community,* 68; Schnackenburg, *Gospel According to St John,* 1:167; Meeks, "Man from Heaven," 70; and Wengst, *Gemeinde,* 32–36.

17. Because of this, as well as a slight preponderance in the manuscripts, the present *pisteuēte* and not the aorist *pisteusēte* may be the correct reading in John 20:31. But the relation of the tenses to the meaning and to John's purpose is complex: cf. Schnackenburg, *Gospel According to St John,* 3:338; Barrett, *Gospel According to St. John,* 134–135, 575; and Brown, *Gospel According to John,* 2:1056.

18. See the studies referred to in n. 3 above.

19. Käsemann, *Testament,* 59–60. Contrast Wengst, *Gemeinde,* 125–128.

20. Käsemann, *Testament,* 19.

21. Cf. Brown, *Community,* 72; and Duke, *Irony,* 152–153.

22. James D. Purvis, "The Fourth Gospel and the Samaritans," *NovT* 17 (1975) 161–198; Wayne A. Meeks, "'Am I a Jew?'— Johannine Christianity and Judaism," *Christianity, Judaism and Other Greco-Roman Cults* (ed. Jacob Neusner), 1:176–178; Cullmann, *Johanneische Kreis,* 39–40, 49–52, and passim; Brown, *Community,* 36–40. There is considerable variation among these positions (and others cited especially by Purvis) regarding the exact extent of Samaritan involvement in the Johannine community and the Fourth Gospel. I would simply note that there likely were Samaritans among the Christians accepted by the Fourth Evangelist, and that he gives us no cause to think that mission to the Samaritans was at an end.

23. So in various ways Brown, *Community,* 55–58; Cullmann, *Johanneische Kreis,* 50; Barrett, *Gospel According to St. John,* 325, 420–421; and Schnackenburg, *Gospel According to St John,* 2:150.

24. Barrett, *Gospel According to St. John,* 426.

25. Albert Curry Winn, *A Sense of Mission: Guidance from the Gospel of John,* 69.

26. Ibid., 70, 72, 74.

27. José Porfirio Miranda, *Being and the Messiah: The Message of St. John,* 101–102.

28. Onuki *(Gemeinde,* 41–45) and Luise Schottroff *(Der Glaubende und die feindliche Welt,* 229–233), despite his disagreement with her regarding the nature of gnostic dualism (Onuki, *Gemeinde,* 52–53), both show that the "world" in the negative sense exists only in its negative response to God's revelatory initiative. Cf. Bultmann, *Gospel of John,* 54–55; Barrett, *Gospel According to St. John,* 161–162; and Schnackenburg, *Gospel According to St John,* 1:255–256.

29. On the relation of John's dualism to his concept of revelation and to the community's self-understanding, see Onuki, *Gemeinde,* 38–62.

30. On this whole subject, see Miranda, *Being and the Messiah,* 96–100.

31. Cf. Onuki, *Gemeinde,* 83–84.

32. Miranda, *Being and the Messiah,* 81–90, 156–202; cf. chapter 6 above.

33. Käsemann, *Testament,* 29–32. Similarly, Bultmann, *Gospel of John,* 693; Brown, *Gospel According to John,* 2:1044; and Lindars, *Gospel of John,* 611.

34. Käsemann, *Testament,* 29, 31; Sandra M. Schneiders, "Women in the Fourth Gospel and the Role of Women in the Contemporary Church," *BTB* 12 (1982) 35–45; and Brown, *Community,* 183–198.

35. Cf. Raymond E. Brown, *The Epistles of John,* 371–374.

36. George W. MacRae, "The Fourth Gospel and *Religionsge-schichte,*" *CBQ* 32 (1970) 13–24. See also Onuki, *Gemeinde,* 19–28.

Bibliography

Barrett, C. K. *The Gospel According to St. John.* 2nd ed. Philadelphia: Westminster Press, 1978.

Bassler, Jouette M. "The Galileans: A Neglected Factor in Johannine Community Research." *CBQ* 43 (1981) 243–257.

Bauer, Walter; William F. Arndt; and F. Wilbur Gingrich. *A Greek-English Lexicon of the New Testament and Other Early Christian Literature.* Chicago: University of Chicago Press, 1957.

Becker, Jürgen. "Aus der Literatur zum Johannesevangelium (1978–1980)." *ThR* 47 (1982) 279–301.

————. "Aus der Literatur zum Johannesevangelium (1978–1980): 2. Fortsetzung." *ThR* 47 (1982) 305–347.

————. "Das Johannesevangelium im Streit der Methoden (1980–1984)." *ThR* 51 (1986) 1–78.

————. "J 3,1–21 als Reflex johanneischer Schuldiskussion." In *Das Wort und die Wörter,* edited by Horst Balz and Siegfried Schulz, 85–95. Stuttgart: Kohlhammer, 1973.

Belleville, Linda. "Born of Water and Spirit." *Trinity Journal,* N.S. 1 (1980) 125–141.

Blank, Josef. "Die Verhandlung vor Pilatus Joh 18,28–19, 16 im Lichte johanneischer Theologie." *BZ,* N.S. 3 (1959) 60–81.

Boff, Leonardo. "Christ's Liberation via Oppression: An Attempt at Theological Construction from the Standpoint of Latin America." In *Frontiers of Theology in Latin America,* edited by Rosino Gibellini, 100–132. Maryknoll, N.Y.: Orbis, Books, 1979.

Borgen, Peder. *Bread from Heaven: An Exegetical Study of the Concept of Manna in the Gospel of John and the Writings of Philo.* NovTSup 10. Leiden: E. J. Brill, 1965.

Bornkamm, Günther. "Die eucharistische Rede im Johannes-Evangelium." *ZNW* 47 (1956) 161–169.

————. "Vorjohanneische Tradition oder nachjohanneische Bearbeitung in der eucharistischen Rede Johannes 6?" In *Geschichte und Glaube,* 2:51–64. *Gesammelte Aufsätze,* vol. 4. BEvT 53. Munich: Chr. Kaiser Verlag, 1971.

Braun, F.-M. "Le Don de Dieu et l'Initiation Chrétienne." *NRT* 86 (1964) 1025–1048.

Brown, Raymond E. *The Community of the Beloved Disciple.* New York: Paulist Press, 1979.

————. *The Epistles of John.* AB 30. Garden City, N.Y.: Doubleday & Co., 1982.

————. "The Eucharist and Baptism in John." In *New Testament Essays,* by Raymond E. Brown, 77–95. New York: Paulist Press, 1965.

————. *The Gospel According to John.* 2 vols. AB 29, 29A. Garden City, N.Y.: Doubleday & Co., 1966, 1970.

————. "The Johannine Sacramentary." In *New Testament Essays,* by Raymond E. Brown, 51–76. New York: Paulist Press, 1965.

Bultmann, Rudolf. *The Gospel of John: A Commentary.* Philadelphia: Westminster Press, 1971.

————. *The History of the Synoptic Tradition.* New York: Harper & Row, 1963.

————. *Theology of the New Testament.* Translated by Kendrick Grobel. Vol. 2. New York: Charles Scribner's Sons, 1955.

Catchpole, David R. *The Trial of Jesus: A Study in the Gospels and Jewish Historiography from 1770 to the Present Day.* SPB 18. Leiden: E. J. Brill, 1971.

Cone, James H. *Black Theology and Black Power.* New York: Seabury Press, 1969.

————. *God of the Oppressed.* New York: Seabury Press, 1975.

Cullmann, Oscar. *Der johanneische Kreis.* Tübingen: J. C. B. Mohr (Paul Siebeck), 1975.

————. *Early Christian Worship.* Translated by A. Stewart Todd and James B. Torrance. Philadelphia: Westminster Press, 1953.

————. *Jesus and the Revolutionaries.* New York: Harper & Row, 1970.

Culpepper, R. Alan. *Anatomy of the Fourth Gospel: A Study in Literary Design.* Philadelphia: Fortress Press, 1983.

Dauer, Anton. *Die Passionsgeschichte im Johannesevangelium: Eine traditionsgeschichtliche und theologische Untersuchung zu Joh 18,1–19,30.* SANT 30. Munich: Kösel-Verlag, 1972.

Dibelius, Martin. *From Tradition to Gospel.* New York: Charles Scribner's Sons, 1935.

Dodd, C. H. *Historical Tradition in the Fourth Gospel.* Cambridge: Cambridge University Press, 1963.

————. *The Interpretation of the Fourth Gospel.* Cambridge: Cambridge University Press, 1953.

Duke, Paul D. *Irony in the Fourth Gospel.* Atlanta: John Knox Press, 1985.

Dunn, J. D. G. "John vi—A Eucharistic Discourse?" *NTS* 17 (1970–1971) 328–338.

Evans, C. F. "The Passion of John." In C. F. Evans, *Explorations in Theology 2,* 50–66. London: SCM Press, 1977.

Fierro, Alfredo. *The Militant Gospel.* Maryknoll, N.Y.: Orbis Books, 1977.

Fortna, Robert T. *The Gospel of Signs: A Reconstruction of the Narrative Source Underlying the Fourth Gospel.* SNTSMS 11. Cambridge: Cambridge University Press, 1970.

Gager, John G. "Social Description and Social Explanation in the Study of

Early Christianity: A Review Essay." In *The Bible and Liberation: Political and Social Hermeneutics,* edited by Norman K. Gottwald, 428–440. Maryknoll, N.Y.: Orbis Books, 1983. Originally in *RelSRev* 5 (1979) 174–180.

Gardner-Smith, P. *Saint John and the Synoptic Gospels.* Cambridge: Cambridge University Press, 1938.

Gottwald, Norman K., ed. *The Bible and Liberation: Political and Social Hermeneutics.* Maryknoll, N.Y.: Orbis Books, 1983.

Haenchen, Ernst. "Jesus vor Pilatus (Joh. 18, 28–29, 15)." In *Gott und Mensch,* by Ernst Haenchen, 144–156. Tübingen: J. C. B. Mohr (Paul Siebeck), 1965. Originally in *TLZ* 85 (1960) 93–102.

———. *John: A Commentary on the Gospel of John.* 2 vols. Hermeneia. Philadelphia: Fortress Press, 1984.

Herzog, Frederick. *Liberation Theology: Liberation in the Light of the Fourth Gospel.* New York: Seabury Press, 1972.

Hodges, Zane C. "Water and Spirit—John 3:5." *BSac* 135 (1978) 206–220.

Hoskyns, E. C., and F. N. Davey. *The Fourth Gospel.* 2nd ed. London: Faber & Faber, 1947.

Howard, W. F. *The Fourth Gospel in Recent Criticism and Interpretation.* 4th ed. revised by C. K. Barrett. London: Epworth Press, 1955.

Hunter, Archibald M. *The Gospel According to John.* Cambridge Bible Commentary. Cambridge: Cambridge University Press, 1965.

Johnson, Thomas F. "Sectarianism and the Johannine Community." *JBL,* forthcoming. Originally read at the Society of Biblical Literature annual meeting, Atlanta, Georgia, November 23, 1986.

de Jonge, Marinus. *Jesus: Stranger from Heaven and Son of God.* SBLSBS 11. Missoula, Mont.: Scholars Press, 1977.

Käsemann, Ernst. *The Testament of Jesus: A Study of the Gospel of John in the Light of Chapter 17.* Philadelphia: Fortress Press, 1968.

Katz, Steven T. "Issues in the Separation of Judaism and Christianity after 70 C.E.: A Reconsideration." *JBL* 103 (1984) 43–76.

Kimelman, Reuven. *"Birkat Ha-Minim* and the Lack of Evidence for an Anti-Christian Jewish Prayer in Late Antiquity." In *Jewish and Christian Self-Definition,* edited by E. P. Sanders, 2:226–244. Philadelphia: Fortress Press, 1981.

Klos, Herbert. *Die Sakramente im Johannesevangelium.* SBS 46. Stuttgart: Katholisches Bibelwerk, 1970.

Köster, Helmut. "Geschichte und Kultus im Johannesevangelium und bei Ignatius von Antiochien." *ZTK* 54 (1957) 56–69.

Kysar, Robert. *The Fourth Evangelist and His Gospel: An Examination of Contemporary Scholarship.* Minneapolis: Augsburg Publishing House, 1975.

———. "The Gospel of John in Current Research." *RelSRev* 9 (1983) 314–323.

Leroy, Herbert. *Rätsel und Missverständnis: Ein Beitrag zur Formgeschichte des Johannesevangeliums.* BBB 30. Bonn: Peter Hanstein, 1968.

Lindars, Barnabas. *Behind the Fourth Gospel.* Studies in Creative Criticism 3. London: SPCK, 1971.

――――. *The Gospel of John.* NCBC. Grand Rapids, Mich.: Wm. B. Eerdmans Publishing Co., 1972.

――――. "John and the Synoptic Gospels: A Test Case." *NTS* 27 (1981) 287–294.

――――. "Word and Sacrament in the Fourth Gospel." *SJT* 29 (1976) 49–63.

Lindemann, Andreas. *Paulus im ältesten Christentum.* BHT 58. Tübingen: J. C. B. Mohr (Paul Siebeck), 1979.

Lohse, Eduard. "Wort und Sakrament im Johannesevangelium." *NTS* 7 (1960–1961) 110–125.

Loisy, Alfred. *Le quatrième évangile.* Paris: Picard, 1903.

MacRae, George W. "The Fourth Gospel and *Religionsgeschichte.*" *CBQ* 32 (1970) 13–24.

Malina, Bruce J. *The Gospel of John in Sociolinguistic Perspective.* Protocol of the Colloquy of the Center for Hermeneutical Studies in Hellenistic and Modern Culture 48. Berkeley, Calif.: Center for Hermeneutical Studies, 1985.

Mantel, Hugo. "The Causes of the Bar Kokba Revolt." *JQR* 58 (1968) 224–242, 274–296.

Martyn, J. Louis. "Glimpses into the History of the Johannine Community." *The Gospel of John in Christian History,* 90–121. New York: Paulist Press, 1978.

――――. *History and Theology in the Fourth Gospel.* 2nd ed. rev. and enl. Nashville: Abingdon Press, 1979.

――――. "Source Criticism and Religionsgeschichte in the Fourth Gospel." In *The Interpretation of John,* edited by John Ashton, 99–121. Issues in Religion and Theology 9. Philadelphia: Fortress Press; London: SPCK, 1986. Originally in *Jesus and Man's Hope,* edited by David G. Buttrick, 1:247–273. Pittsburgh: Pittsburgh Theological Seminary, 1970.

Matsunaga, Kikuo. "Is John's Gospel Anti-Sacramental?—A New Solution in the Light of the Evangelist's Milieu." *NTS* 27 (1981) 516–524.

Mays, Benjamin E. *The Negro's God, as Reflected in His Literature.* Boston: Chapman & Grimes, 1938.

Meeks, Wayne A. "'Am I a Jew?'—Johannine Christianity and Judaism." *Christianity, Judaism and Other Greco-Roman Cults: Studies for Morton Smith at Sixty,* edited by Jacob Neusner, 1:163–186. 4 vols. SJLA 12. Leiden: E. J. Brill, 1975.

――――. *The First Urban Christians: The Social World of the Apostle Paul.* New Haven, Conn.: Yale University Press, 1983.

――――. "The Man from Heaven in Johannine Sectarianism." *JBL* 91 (1972) 44–72.

――――. *The Prophet-King: Moses Traditions and the Johannine Christology.* NovTSup 14. Leiden: E. J. Brill, 1967.

Michel, M. "Nicodème ou le non-lieu de la vérité." *RevScRel* 55 (1981) 227–236.

Miranda, José Porfirio. *Being and the Messiah: The Message of St. John.* Maryknoll, N.Y.: Orbis Books, 1977.

Murphy, Frederick J. *"2 Baruch* and the Romans." *JBL* 104 (1985) 663–669.

Nations, Archie L. "Jewish Persecution of Christians in the Gospel of John." Paper read at the Society of Biblical Literature annual meeting, Atlanta, Georgia, November 23, 1986.

Neusner, Jacob. *A Life of Yohanan ben Zakkai ca. 1–80 C.E.* SPB 6. 2nd ed. Leiden: E. J. Brill, 1970.

————. *From Politics to Piety: The Emergence of Pharisaic Judaism.* Englewood Cliffs, N.J.: Prentice-Hall, 1973.

Neyrey, Jerome H. "John III—A Debate over Johannine Epistemology and Christology." *NovT* 23 (1981) 115–127.

Onuki, Takashi. *Gemeinde und Welt im Johannesevangelium: Ein Beitrag zur Frage nach der theologischen und pragmatischen Funktion des johanneischen "Dualismus."* WMANT 56. Neukirchen-Vluyn: Neukirchener Verlag, 1984.

Pagels, Elaine H. *The Johannine Gospel in Gnostic Exegesis: Heracleon's Commentary on John.* SBLMS 17. Nashville: Abingdon Press, 1973.

Pamment, Margaret. "John 3:5." *NovT* 25 (1983) 189–190.

Paschal, R. Wade, Jr. "Sacramental Symbolism and Physical Imagery in the Gospel of John." *Tyndale Bulletin* 32 (1981) 151–176.

Payot, Christian. "L'interprétation johannique du ministère de Jean-Baptiste (Jean I)." *Foi et vie* 68 (1969) 21–37.

de la Potterie, Ignace. "Jésus roi et juge d'après Jn 19,13." *Bib* 41 (1960) 217–247.

————. " 'To Be Born Again of Water and the Spirit'—The Baptismal Text of John 3,5." In *The Christian Lives by the Spirit,* by Ignace de la Potterie and Stanislaus Lyonnet, 1–36. Staten Island, N.Y.: Alba House, 1971. Translation of *La vie selon l'Esprit,* Paris: Editions du Cerf, 1968. Originally in *Sciences ecclésiastiques* 14 (1962) 417–443.

Purvis, James D. "The Fourth Gospel and the Samaritans." *NovT* 17 (1975) 161–198.

Rensberger, David K. "As the Apostle Teaches: The Development of the Use of Paul's Letters in Second-Century Christianity." Ph.D. dissertation, Yale University, 1981.

Richter, Georg. "Die Gefangennahme Jesu nach dem Johannesevangelium (18,1–12)." In *Studien zum Johannesevangelium,* by Georg Richter, 74–87. Biblische Untersuchungen 13. Regensburg: Pustet, 1977. Originally in *BibLeb* 10 (1969) 26–39.

————. "Präsentische und futurische Eschatologie im 4. Evangelium." In *Studien zum Johannesevangelium,* by Georg Richter, 346–382. Biblische Untersuchungen 13. Regensburg: Pustet, 1977. Originally in *Gegenwart und kommendes Reich,* edited by Peter Fiedler and Dieter Zeller, 117–152. SBB. Stuttgart, 1975.

————. "Zum gemeindebildenden Element in den johanneischen Schriften." In *Studien zum Johannesevangelium,* by Georg Richter, 383–414. Biblische Untersuchungen 13. Regensburg: Pustet, 1977. Originally in *Kirche im Werden: Studien zum Thema Amt und Gemeinde im Neuen Testament,* edited by Josef Hainz, 253–292. Paderborn, 1976.

————. "Zur Formgeschichte und literarischen Einheit von Joh 6,31–58." In

Studien zum Johannesevangelium, by Georg Richter, 88–119. Biblische Untersuchungen 13. Regensburg: Pustet, 1977. Originally in *ZNW* 60 (1969) 21–55.

Robertson, A. T. *A Grammar of the Greek New Testament in the Light of Historical Research.* Nashville: Broadman Press, 1934.

Robinson, D. W. B. "Born of Water and Spirit." *Reformed Theological Review* (Australia) 25 (1966) 15–23.

Robinson, John A. T. "The New Look on the Fourth Gospel." In *Twelve New Testament Studies,* by John A. T. Robinson, 94–106. SBT 34. Naperville, Ill.: Alec R. Allenson, 1962.

Ruckstuhl, Eugen. *Die literarische Einheit des Johannesevangeliums.* Studia Friburgensia, N.S. 3. Freiburg: Paulus, 1951.

Schlier, Heinrich. "Jesus und Pilatus nach dem Johannesevangelium." In *Die Zeit der Kirche: Exegetische Aufsätze und Vorträge,* by Heinrich Schlier, 56–74. 4th ed. Freiburg: Herder, 1966.

———. "The State According to the New Testament." In *The Relevance of the New Testament,* by Heinrich Schlier, 215–238. Freiburg and New York: Herder & Herder, 1968.

Schnackenburg, Rudolf. *The Gospel According to St John.* 3 vols. New York: Crossroad Publishing Co., 1982.

Schneiders, Sandra M. "Reflections on Commitment in the Gospel According to John." *BTB* 8 (1978) 40–48.

———. "Women in the Fourth Gospel and the Role of Women in the Contemporary Church." *BTB* 12 (1982) 35–45.

Schottroff, Luise. *Der Glaubende und die feindliche Welt.* WMANT 37. Neukirchen-Vluyn: Neukirchener Verlag, 1970.

Schürer, Emil. *The History of the Jewish People in the Age of Jesus Christ (175 B.C.–A.D. 135).* Revised edition by Geza Vermes and Fergus Millar. Vol. 1. Edinburgh: T. & T. Clark, 1973.

Schürmann, Heinz. "Joh 6,51c—ein Schlüssel zur grossen johanneischen Brotrede." *BZ,* N.S. 2 (1958) 244–262.

Schweizer, Eduard. "Das johanneische Zeugnis vom Herrenmahl." *EvTh* 12 (1953) 341–363.

Scroggs, Robin. "The Earliest Christian Communities as Sectarian Movement." In *Christianity, Judaism and Other Greco-Roman Cults: Studies for Morton Smith at Sixty,* edited by Jacob Neusner, 2:1–23. 4 vols. SJLA 12. Leiden: E. J. Brill, 1975.

———. "The Sociological Interpretation of the New Testament." In *The Bible and Liberation: Political and Social Hermeneutics,* edited by Norman K. Gottwald, 337–356. Maryknoll, N.Y.: Orbis Books, 1983. Originally in *NTS* 26 (1980) 164–179.

Segovia, Fernando. "The Love and Hatred of Jesus and Johannine Sectarianism." *CBQ* 43 (1981) 258–272.

———. *Love Relationships in the Johannine Tradition: Agapê/Agapan in I John and the Fourth Gospel.* SBLDS 58. Chico, Calif.: Scholars Press, 1982.

Smallwood, E. Mary. *The Jews under Roman Rule.* SJLA 20. Leiden: E. J. Brill, 1976.

Smith, D. Moody. "Johannine Christianity." In *Johannine Christianity:*

Essays on Its Setting, Sources, and Theology, by D. Moody Smith, 1–36. Columbia, S.C.: University of South Carolina Press, 1984. Originally in *NTS* 21 (1976) 222–248.

———. "John and the Synoptics: Some Dimensions of the Problem." In *Johannine Christianity: Essays on Its Setting, Sources, and Theology,* by D. Moody Smith, 145–172. Columbia, S.C.: University of South Carolina Press, 1984. Originally in *NTS* 26 (1980) 425–444.

———. "The Milieu of the Johannine Miracle Source." In *Johannine Christianity: Essays on Its Setting, Sources, and Theology,* by D. Moody Smith, 62–79. Columbia, S.C.: University of South Carolina Press, 1984. Originally in *Jews, Greeks, and Christians,* edited by Robert Hamerton-Kelly and Robin Scroggs, 164–180. Leiden: E. J. Brill, 1976.

———. "The Presentation of Jesus in the Fourth Gospel." In *Johannine Christianity: Essays on Its Setting, Sources, and Theology,* by D. Moody Smith, 175–189. Columbia, S.C.: University of South Carolina Press, 1984. Originally in *Interpretation* 31 (1977) 367–378.

———. "The Setting and Shape of a Johannine Narrative Source." In *Johannine Christianity: Essays on Its Setting, Sources, and Theology,* by D. Moody Smith, 80–93. Columbia, S.C.: University of South Carolina Press, 1984. Originally in *JBL* 95 (1976) 231–241.

———. "The Sources of the Gospel of John." In *Johannine Christianity: Essays on Its Setting, Sources, and Theology,* by D. Moody Smith, 56–61. Columbia, S.C.: University of South Carolina Press, 1984. Originally in *NTS* 10 (1964) 336–351.

Smith, Morton. "Palestinian Judaism in the First Century." In *Israel: Its Role in Civilization,* edited by Moshe Davis, 67–81. New York: Jewish Theological Seminary of America, 1956.

Spriggs, D. G. "Meaning of 'Water' in John 3⁵." *ExpTim* 85 (1973–1974) 149–150.

Temple, Sydney. "A Key to the Composition of the Fourth Gospel." *JBL* 80 (1961) 222–232.

Theological Commission of the National Conference of Black Churchmen. "Black Theology in 1976." In *Black Theology: A Documentary History, 1966–1979,* edited by Gayraud S. Wilmore and James H. Cone, 342–343. Maryknoll, N.Y.: Orbis Books, 1979.

Thielman, Frank S. "Inside or Outside? An Assessment of Recent Research on the Purpose of the Fourth Gospel." Paper read at the Society of Biblical Literature Southeast Regional meeting, Chattanooga, Tennessee, March 21, 1986.

Thyen, Hartwig. "Aus der Literatur zum Johannesevangelium (1. Fortsetzung)." *ThR* 39 (1974) 222–252.

———. "Aus der Literatur zum Johannesevangelium (2. Fortsetzung)." *ThR* 40 (1975) 289–330.

———. "Aus der Literatur zum Johannesevangelium (3. Fortsetzung)." *ThR* 42 (1977) 221–270.

———. "Aus der Literatur zum Johannesevangelium (4. Fortsetzung)." *ThR* 43 (1978) 328–359.

————. "Aus der Literatur zum Johannesevangelium (5. Fortsetzung)." *ThR* 44 (1979) 97–134.

————. "Entwicklungen innerhalb der johanneischen Theologie und Kirche im Spiegel von Joh. 21 und der Lieblingsjüngertexte des Evangeliums." In *L'Evangile de Jean: Sources, rédaction, théologie,* edited by Marinus de Jonge, 259–299. BETL 44. Gembloux: Duculot; Louvain: University Press, 1977.

Wengst, Klaus. *Bedrängte Gemeinde und verherrlichter Christus: Der historische Ort des Johannesevangeliums als Schlüssel zu seiner Interpretation.* Biblisch-Theologische Studien 5. 2nd ed. Neukirchen-Vluyn: Neukirchener Verlag, 1983.

Whitacre, Rodney A. *Johannine Polemic: The Role of Tradition and Theology.* SBLDS 67. Chico, Calif.: Scholars Press, 1982.

Wilckens, Ulrich. "Der eucharistische Abschnitt der johanneischen Rede vom Lebensbrot (Joh 6, 51c–58)." In *Neues Testament und Kirche* (Festschrift Rudolf Schnackenburg), edited by Joachim Gnilka, 220–248. Freiburg: Herder, 1974.

Wiles, Maurice F. *The Spiritual Gospel: The Interpretation of the Fourth Gospel in the Early Church.* Cambridge: Cambridge University Press, 1960.

Wilkens, Wilhelm. "Das Abendmahlszeugnis im vierten Evangelium." *EvTh* 18 (1958) 354–370.

————. *Die Entstehungsgeschichte des vierten Evangeliums.* Zollikon: Evangelischer Verlag, 1958.

Wilson, Bryan R. *Magic and the Millennium: A Sociological Study of Religious Movements of Protest Among Tribal and Third-World Peoples.* New York: Harper & Row, 1973.

Wilson, Jeffrey. "The Integrity of John 3:22–36." *JSNT* 10 (1981) 34–41.

Winn, Albert Curry. *A Sense of Mission: Guidance from the Gospel of John.* Philadelphia: Westminster Press, 1981.

Witherington, Ben. "The Waters of Birth: John 3.5 and 1 John 5.6–8." Paper read at the Society of Biblical Literature annual meeting, Atlanta, Georgia, November 23, 1986.

Woll, D. Bruce. *Johannine Christianity in Conflict: Authority, Rank, and Succession in the First Farewell Discourse.* SBLDS 60. Chico, Calif.: Scholars Press, 1981.

Zorilla, Hugo C. "The Feast of Liberation of the Oppressed: A Rereading of John 7:1–10:21." *Mission Focus* 13 (1985) 21–24.

Subject Index

abiding in Jesus, 78-81, 99

above, be from, 52, 58, 59, 98, 116, 119, 120, 137; *see also* birth from above

Abraham, 56, 125

adherence to community of faith, 58, 69, 78, 81, 113-114, 130

Akiba, Rabbi, 89

allegiance to Jesus, 45, 99, 116, 131

'am ha-aretz, 49

Anabaptists, 129

baptism, 57-61, 64-70, 81, 113, 148

Bar Kokhba, 89

Barabbas, 93, 96, 99, 116, 131

Barrett, C. K., 53, 146

2 Baruch, 88

Becker, Jürgen, 23, 53

believing in Jesus, 38-39, 48, 52-53, 60-61, 79, 113, 147-148, 151

Benediction against Heretics, 22, 26

birth from above, 38, 55-60, 66-70, 113-114, 116, 120, 137, 148, 152; *see also* baptism

blacks, 108, 115, 121-122

black theology, 108, 121-123

Blank, Josef, 97

blind man, 41-49, 69, 79, 90, 129, 142

Borgen, Peder, 71

Bornkamm, Günther, 72, 74

boundaries, communal, 61, 65, 68-70, 77-78, 80-81, 113

Brown, Raymond, 21, 22, 27, 28, 40-41, 49, 53, 67, 73, 140

Bultmann, Rudolf, 18, 19, 20, 21, 38, 53, 54, 57, 64, 66, 68, 73, 135

Caesar, 95, 96, 98-99, 116-118

Caiaphas, 95

Christianity, contemporary, 115-116, 138-143, 146-147, 150-152

Christian-Jewish relations, postbiblical, 126, 139

Christology, 23-24, 28, 40, 45-46, 56, 58, 60-61, 65, 68, 71-81 passim, 118-123, 127, 140-143, 149

church, 115, 117, 129, 131, 136, 141-143

Clement of Alexandria, 16

community, Johannine: alienation of, 27-28, 81, 99, 119-120, 122, 142; background of, 25, 49; conflict with synagogue, 22, 24, 25-27, 43, 45, 48, 79, 119; as counterculture, 45, 136, 150; egalitarianism, 130, 148-149; as eschatological community, 127-129, 147-148, 150; and gospel of John, 21-22, 28-29, 144-145; history of, 22-24, 25-29; and Johannine Christology, 25, 28, 46, 80-81, 119-121, 140; and John the Baptist, 60-61; love in, 79-81, 127, 128, 129; as oppressed, 110-111, 118, 120-121, 127-128, 131, 137-138; and secret Christians, 41, 60-61, 68-69, 114; sectarianism, 27-28, 81, 119, 124-126, 130, 135-136, 138; symbolized by blind man, 41-42, 45-47; symbolized by Jesus, 28, 38, 90, 96, 120-121

Cone, James, 121, 122

confession of Jesus, 25-26, 39-41, 45-48, 58, 59-61, 68-69, 79, 81,

Scripture Index